# Collaboration: Artists & Architects

The Centennial Project of
The Architectural League

# COLLAB

*Barbaralee Diamonstein,*
*Editor*

*Vincent Scully, Paul Goldberger,*
*Stephen Prokopoff, Jonathan Barnett,*
*Jane Livingston*

# ARTISTS & ARCHITECTS

# ORATION

Emilio Ambasz & Michael Meritet
James Freed & Alice Aycock
Frank Gehry & Richard Serra
Michael Graves & Lennart Anderson
Hugh Hardy & Jack Beal and
Sondra Freckelton

Richard Meier & Frank Stella
Charles Moore & Alice Wingwall
Cesar Pelli & William Bailey
Robert A.M. Stern & Robert Graham
Stanley Tigerman & Richard Haas
Susana Torre & Charles Simonds

WHITNEY LIBRARY OF DESIGN
an imprint of Watson-Guptill Publications/New York

Copyright © 1981 by The Architectural League

First Published 1981 in New York
by the Whitney Library of Design,
an imprint of Watson-Guptill Publications,
a division of Billboard Publications, Inc.,
1515 Broadway, New York, N.Y. 10036

**Library of Congress Cataloging
in Publication Data**

Main entry under title:
Collaboration, artists and architects.
    Includes index.
    1. Decoration and ornament, Architectural.
I. Diamonstein, Barbaralee. II. Architectural
League of New York.
NA3320.C64        729        80-27526
ISBN 0-8230-7126-X

Manufactured in U.S.A.

First Printing, 1981

Edited by Sharon Lee Ryder and Susan Davis
for the Whitney Library of Design
Designed by Massimo Vignelli
Graphic production by Ellen Greene
Set in 12 point Century Expanded

## Sponsor's Statement

*George Weissman*
*Chairman of the Board*
*Philip Morris Incorporated*

What shapes our cities and communities shapes our spirit and well-being. This implicit relationship underlines the inherent value of such projects as The Architectural League Centennial Celebration, its exhibition, and this publication.

American corporations are increasingly aware that art and architecture complement each other and that together they form the physical and aesthetic structures of our social character.

Philip Morris has experienced first hand the liberating and creative powers which art and architecture possess. In the early 1960s, we were looking for a way "to show our people we were not shackled by the past nor afraid of change."

A young architect, Ulrich Franzen, spoke to us about "creative atmospheres" and "stimulating environments." We told him to go ahead and redesign our corporate headquarters. We didn't know it at the time, but this decision marked the genesis of both our architectural program and our corporate art program. In tandem, they have become integral features of the creative corporate personality of the company that they have helped mold.

Committed interest in art and architecture by companies like Philip Morris has evolved from a growing, practical, and sometimes costly sense of social responsibility toward the nation and the communities in which we work and live. Probably no creative endeavor shapes our social environment and our image of the world more intimately or more profoundly than architecture.

These are strange, unsettling, and uncertain times for architecture, but we still rely on it not to scar our spirit or entomb our hopes with mass-produced banality and pervasive shabbiness. Rather, we have every reason to believe that architecture, in natural and essential partnership with art, will construct great stages of harmonious and pleasing sets on which we may enact, with common grace and infinite variety of style, a more rewarding and more humane life.

# Contents

# Foreword

*By Jonathan Barnett*
*President of The Architectural League*
*of New York, 1977–1981*

When The Architectural League was founded in 1881, one of its principal purposes was to bring architects and other artists together. America was in the midst of the Arts and Crafts Movement, which promoted the collaboration of architects with artists and craftsmen, including such specialists as stone and wood carvers, fabric designers, and artisans in stained glass. The country was also at the beginning of what has been called the American Renaissance, which was attempting to revive the relationships that had once existed among architecture and the "fine arts," painting and sculpture.

Over the years since 1881 the relationships among the arts have gone through several radical transformations. For a long time, collaboration among architecture and the other arts has been almost nonexistent. Recently, however, there have been indications of a new potential for such collaboration. Artists have been showing an interest in what is described as "environmental" art, and architects have begun to make experiments with ornament and elaboration.

As part of the activities to mark its Centennial, The Architectural League decided to organize an exhibition and book that would focus attention on the history of the collaboration among architects and other artists, discuss what has been happening recently when artists and architects work together, and show the possibilities that could exist for collaboration in the future.

We asked Barbaralee Diamonstein to turn this interesting—but highly speculative—concept into reality, and I don't know anyone else who could have done it. It was Barbaralee who gave this project shape and direction from her knowledge of the worlds of art and architecture. It was she who acted as the catalytic agent to get the chemistry of collaboration going, and it was she who made sure that each of the participants did his or her best work. It was also Barbaralee Diamonstein's skill in communicating complex artistic issues to the public as curator and editor that put all the pieces of the project together.

The League is grateful to all the participants for their interest and enthusiasm. Vincent Scully has given us an extraordinary historical synthesis of major relationships among architecture and the other arts; Paul Goldberger, Stephen Prokopoff, and Jane Livingston have contributed valuable critical perspectives; and the artists and architects we have commissioned have been willing to define their own tasks and then carry them out with distinction. Massimo Vignelli, the exhibition and book designer, has, as usual, made the difficult look easy and the complex simple to understand.

We are grateful to the National Endowment for the Arts (NEA) and particularly to Michael Pittas, the director of the NEA's Design Arts Program, who was willing to back this enterprise at a formative stage. It was Philip Morris Incorporated that matched the NEA commitment and thus made the whole exhibition possible, and we are pleased that Philip Morris had faith that we could complete such an ambitious undertaking. We have also received a contribution from the New York State Council on the Arts, and it is their annual grant that helps keep The Architectural League in operation.

# Acknowledgments

There are many dedicated people whose efforts in behalf of this project have earned my deep thanks—more than I can possibly single out here. But there are three whose contributions were so indispensable that I must mention them: Jonathan Barnett, president of The Architectural League, whose encouragement and friendship proved the impetus for the book and the exhibit; Massimo Vignelli, the remarkable designer of both; and Sharon Lee Ryder of the Whitney Library of Design, who gave generously of her time and energy. Obviously, none of this would have been possible without the wholehearted support, conceptual and economic, given by our sponsors, and the enlightened manner in which they gave it. My genuine appreciation to George Weissman, Chairman of the Board of Philip Morris Incorporated and to Michael Pittas, Charles Zucker, and Lance Brown of the National Endowment for the Arts. And thanks, too, to Helen Chillman, Librarian of the Slide and Photographic Collection of Yale University; Susan Davis of the Whitney Library of Design; and Carl Spielvogel, who was able to envision the project before it was transformed into reality.
*Barbaralee Diamonstein*

# Introduction

*By Barbaralee Diamonstein*

*Michelangelo,* Creation of
Adam, *ceiling, Sistine Chapel,*
*1508–1512.*

In 1977 Jonathan Barnett, the president of The
Architectural League, came to me with the request
that I direct the League's Centennial project. After
lengthy discussions, we agreed that a worthy
project would be for me to develop some means of
assessing the state of collaboration between
architects and other artists and of exploring how
such collaboration could be increased in the future.

It was an interesting moment for such a
suggestion for two reasons in particular. First, the
League was founded in 1881 with the expressed aim
of encouraging architects to work closely with
sculptors and painters. Second, after many years
during which that aim was more often frustrated
than fulfilled, we seem to have arrived at a moment
when architects are once again seriously considering
factors like decoration, psychological impact, and
historical resonance in their work. For half a
century or so, the profession had been dominated by
an austere and all too pedantic Modernism that
brooked no departures from its dogma. But now
architecture is, in effect, being liberated, and
architects need no longer fear that they will be
accused of "violating the spirit of the age" if they
work into their project a mural, or a stained glass
panel, or a sympathetic sculpture, or even a touch
of pure whimsy. At the same time, some painters
and sculptors seem to be moving toward art that is
a part of the whole environment or that actively
seeks to reshape the environment.

Coinciding with these developments, there has
also been an increasing movement toward making
art an integral part of public buildings, through
official government programs that set aside a small
part of the total construction and design budget for
works of art. Unfortunately, the results have often
been disappointing. Some of the art was simply
second rate, or even when it was of high quality, it
did not seem an integral part of the building—the
sculpture seemed merely to have been placed in a
convenient courtyard, the painting simply hung on a
long expanse of wall. But the basic idea is an
important one, entirely consonant with the League's
original goal and with the concept that informs this
Centennial project.

When The Architectural League was young,
artists and architects could look to the example of

Richardson's Trinity Church in Boston with its paintings and glass by John LaFarge or to the Boston Public Library by McKim, Mead, & White with mural paintings by such artists as Puvis de Chavannes, Edwin Austin Abbey, and John Singer Sargent. The Boston Library also made extensive use of traditional crafts such as stone carving and the creation of wrought-iron gates and lanterns. In 1892 and 1893 Chicago played host to the World's Columbian Exposition, a project that assembled such a glittering company that the sculptor Augustus Saint-Gaudens was supposed to have observed to the architect Daniel Burnham: "Look here, old fellow, do you realize that this is the greatest meeting of artists since the fifteenth century?"

The 1880s and 1890s were a self-confident time, a time when artists and architects thought they knew what their art was and shared a common ground of understanding on which to base their collaboration. That spirit of mutuality was soon to fade, however, if not to disappear entirely. So it is appropriate that The Architectural League should commemorate its Centennial by helping to redefine and rekindle the concept of collaboration among the arts. This book is one part of the effort; so is the major exhibition bearing the same title. Both the exhibit and book will, I hope, achieve a number of things: help to illuminate the historic relationship between architecture and its allied arts; trace the uneven progress of that relationship in the United States during the last century; describe the complexities of the present, still somewhat strained relationship; and chart some possible directions for the future. Above all, I hope the book and exhibit will demonstrate to a wider public the point that architecture, so often undervalued or, worse, totally ignored, is in many respects the paramount modern art, the one that can and does embrace *all* the arts.

Vincent Scully has contributed an important essay that reaffirms collaboration between the arts as a central theme in the history of art and not the optional "extra" it has sometimes seemed to be in recent years. Paul Goldberger's cogent description of collaboration in the arts since 1945 traces our recent history and gives us a point of departure for Jane Livingston's provocative speculations on the possible future of such artistic collaboration. Stephen Prokopoff has contributed an account of a significant subplot to our story, the efforts of the federal General Services Administration that have led to the expenditure of $6 million for art in nearly 200 federal projects.

Another important part of the League's Centennial project has been to commission actual collaborations. Eleven teams were formed. Each began with an architect, who then selected an artist, or artists, to work with him or her. The teams collaborated on proposals that were supposed to strike a delicate balance between the visionary and the pragmatic—or at least the remotely plausible. Some of the teams functioned quite smoothly. Others, not surprisingly, proved to be less than compatible, at least for a while, though almost all did ultimately get together.

It has often been said that true collaboration can only occur when the architect and the artist are the same person. I believe that we have proved that there are exceptions and have ended up with eleven significant examples of the possibilities of collaboration, although it would be too optimistic to describe them as prototypes. Jonathan Barnett has contributed a thoughtful essay in which he attempts to categorize the eleven projects and assess their significance.

From this experience I have emerged with a new appreciation for both the potential of collaboration between architects and other artists and an increased awareness of its inherent difficulties. If architects and artists are alike in sharing a sense of certitude about their work, in priding themselves on possessing a singular vision, they are about as different as can be in their ways of achieving their goals. Perhaps it is this dissimilarity of method that has been at the root of the historical difficulty in achieving genuine collaboration between artists and architects. Architecture has always been something of a team effort, Ayn Rand's vision of the architect as the last embattled individualist notwithstanding. Architecture is a discipline involving many minds and hands, an ongoing exchange of ideas and skills. Paradoxically, because so much of architecture is a team enterprise, many architects develop strong points of view in order to shape their work and do it well. Painting and sculpture, on the other hand, have traditionally called for solitary, often totally isolated, endeavor. Since the late nineteenth century this isolation seems to have increased. More and more, the visual arts have been concerned with their own forms, so much so that works almost seem to require inert or totally neutral surroundings: just consider some of the really large-scale paintings and sculptures of recent years.

Some artists have even sought to design entire environments rather than objects. In any event, most contemporary painters and sculptors are unalterably opposed to creating anything that might be considered subordinate decoration. At the same time, architects have gone their own way and have aimed increasingly at creating pure aesthetic experiences that can exist on their own terms, free of other embellishment—visual and spatial compositions of lines and forms, enclosures and expanses. Distilled, the difference is in functionalism: architecture's intrinsic relation *to* society, and art's freedom *from* it.

Asking artists and architects, with their differences in perspective and in the recent history of their arts, to collaborate with each other was an audacious enterprise. Collaboration forces a new role on the artist who not only is used to working alone but whose work is often a detached, idiosyncratic comment—or attack—on society. The architect is more used to collaboration but is very much accustomed to being in charge. Being part of a true cooperative partnership is a new role for the architect as well. Yet the members of our eleven teams persevered admirably in their attempts to overcome the professional and psychological barriers that obstruct the growth of respect or, for that matter, sympathy.

One of the architect participants, Emilio Ambasz, commented ruefully on the difficulties of creative exchange when he pointed out that the word "labor" is buried within the word "collaboration." But it is a labor well worth undertaking, one that, as Vincent Scully shows us, architects and artists have been denying for too long. There are risks involved, major risks, but I think we have demonstrated that they are justified. Above all, we believe that the *process* is important. That eleven teams of

architects and artists have been through this process is significant in itself. Both architects and artists have individual creative demands and a desire to prevail. By engaging in the process of working together, whatever the difficulties (and there are many), members of both professions benefit. None can remain untouched, and I daresay their next collaboration will reflect their recent experience. By encouraging practiced solo voices to forget their training and experience and inclination in order to work in harmony, we may enhance the outlooks of both, we may accelerate the process of fermentation, we may bring about a heightened concern for creating more humane environments. In short, we may achieve a happy outcome—and one that need not be the exception. But it will require the utmost effort to make such results the rule. Not only must singular and independent minds cooperate, but they must bring together two allied fields in a unified form.

For all concerned, especially the architects and artists of our eleven teams, this entire project was a labor of love rather than of commerce. I hope they derived some special satisfaction from the enterprise that compensates for how generously they gave of their talent, energy, and ideas. All were completely committed to the theory that animated the entire project: that architecture and art, after their long separation, are again converging; that the two may sometimes collide, but with patient encouragement may more often come together in fruitful collaboration; and that both professions—and we, the public, they are meant to serve—will benefit from the process.

# Part 1

# The Past

# Part 1

# The Past

# Architecture, Sculpture, and Painting: Environment, Act, and Illusion

*By Vincent Scully*

It is a mistake to base judgments about architecture upon criteria which are concerned with architecture alone. To do so is to assess the present state of architecture and to chart out courses for its future on grounds which are in fact too narrow, because architecture is not an isolated art. It is only part of one large human art, indeed of what must be regarded as the fundamental art, which is the shaping of the physical environment and of living in it. All the physical arts (a better term than "visual arts") are aimed toward the fulfillment of those two complementary needs. They are thus one art, of which the functions of the major parts may roughly be articulated as follows: through the art of architecture human beings create an environment for themselves; they shape a space. Through the art of sculpture human beings populate that environment, that space, with their own creatures, embodiments of their own perception of the quality of being alive, which is above all the quality of being potentially able to gesture or to act. Through the art of painting human beings create the illusion of every conceivable kind of environment and of every kind of action in relation to those environments. Painting is the art which, as Josef Albers, the incomparable teacher of abstract art, put it, "makes us see what isn't there." All the arts of illusion, from television to holography, are therefore encompassed by it. It is the freest of all the arts, the most able to explore the character of imagined environments and of new modes of action. Often in history, once painting has discovered its way, it has been the first of the arts to indicate the route that the other arts, especially architecture, were soon to travel.

We therefore cannot think about the present and future of architecture without thinking about all the other arts as well. All the great modern architects, those most concerned with creating their own imagined environment, have known this and have reacted to it in one way or another. Wright always had the other arts in mind, and he consistently tried to subjugate them to, or to weave them into, one architectural system. Le Corbusier, on the other hand, tried to employ the freer methods of painting and sculpture in the making of architectural form. Mies tried to create his luminous, weightless environments with the presence of sculpture and, secondarily, of painting always the essential criterion in his mind. Right now, in 1981, with the relaxation of the special grip upon our imaginations which these architects exercised and with the catastrophe to the environment as a whole which the Modern Movement brought about now plain to our eyes, architects and critics are faced with several fundamental questions relative to the future of their art. One of those questions relates to the problem of tradition. How far, for example, can tradition be called to our aid at present? Can we, more specifically, revive the academic tradition of classical form? Can we, as Allan Greenberg and others would like to do, employ Renaissance and Baroque design once more—straight and without parody—and create an environment with it? If we consider that question in purely architectural terms, we find that there is no logical way in which it can be answered in the negative. Questions of economy, of constructional methods, of program and technology, once analyzed, in fact create no barrier whatever to its accomplishment. Even ornament is possible, however we may wish it. We are left with the uneasy feeling, which we ascribe to a holdover of Modern prejudice in us, that there must somehow be more than adaptation of the past open to us. There must be something new. Despite our revulsion against the International Style's destruction of our cities through its hatred of tradition, we still instinctively tend to recoil from a straight revival of the classical past. The nineteenth-century vernacular is another matter. It has been revived in the work of the most progressive architects and is wholly alive once more. Function, structure, and propriety indicate its use in many cases, especially in domestic architecture, and the inevitable rise of considerations relative to energy will only confirm its revival. But classical architecture, correctly assembled at urban scale, with the full panoply of ornamental detail and of sculpture and painting of the kind that is appropriate to it—can that be? Collaborative problems, aiming toward a positive solution to that question, were the yearly gala events of Beaux-Arts architectural education. I remember that they continued on at Yale for a long while under the Modern regime of the late forties and early fifties. Teams of architects, painters, and sculptors got together. By that time, though, nobody knew what to do, because nobody knew any longer what his special role was meant to be—what his part of the art was supposed to contribute. So everything came out as arty blobs, prehistoric caverns without the animals or the cosmic signs. If we are to have classical architecture, we must start with the premise that we must have collaborative problems once again. If so, we must first decide what the arts are and what they do. There is no better place to start than on the Campidoglio in Rome, where Michelangelo pushed his buildings back at a diagonal to show that architecture is, supremely, space and then placed the Roman equestrian statue of Marcus Aurelius in it to act out, through its gesture, the creation of that space by human action (1). There could be no clearer demonstration of architecture as environment and of sculpture as act. Between the two the world is shaped for human behavior and is made to describe and encourage it.

*1*

*1 Piazza del Campidoglio, Rome, 16th century and later. (This photograph was chosen despite the fact that it was taken before Michelangelo's project for a dynamic pavement pattern was finally realized. Of all extant examples, it seems to show best the actual volume of the space.)*

**A**rchitecture, therefore, is an affair not primarily of individual buildings but of the entire constructed environment from farms to cities. Its first component is the natural world, in Rome almost entirely covered over but heaving up just the same in the seven hills and culminating on the summit of the Capitoline. That component we experience physically, that is, empathetically, as it lifts and subsides, and associationally, as our cultural coding directs us. We experience it in itself and in terms of its human connections. If we know the history of Rome, the experience of the Capitoline is almost unbearably poignant, as, after centuries of deprivation, the Renaissance symbolically takes over the center of Rome's civic power once more. If we don't know our history, it all means less. Thus we experience even nature most fully the more we know, from geological information to historical fact. The same is much more intensely the case with human constructions, because in them we are dealing directly with human intentions as well. We must experience them in relation to nature and in relation to each other. On the Campidoglio we feel the buildings pushed back; we feel the statue push them and then ride up into the volume of space between them. This is empathy. Is it culturally coded? Probably so, but surely more broadly than associationism. So we feel the domes rise. We know they are churches. In an American context they would more likely be government buildings. Each affects us differently. We are squeezed between the palazzi down below, can read the floor levels and sense the restricted scale and so, by contrast, the great bloom of space on the summit of the hill. We will always feel this physically long after the history of Rome is forgotten and its original cultural meaning obscured. Empathy may therefore be regarded as the most essential fact of our experience of a work of art. Other meanings, involving association, may pour in and out of it as the culture of the viewer changes. Such meanings are always multiple anyway and are not limited by the artist's intentions, of which the work of art is never the simple sum. A system of linguistic analysis, like that in vogue among the present crop of semiologists, which reduces the physical arts to the conveying of information through signs is thus faulty, because it is secondary and partial. It ignores the major vehicle of meaning, which is physical experience. But the two modes are also inextricably interwoven. There is no form which is void of associations, just as there can be no meaning without form. Hence knowledge and experience reinforce each other.

So with sculpture. Marcus Aurelius looms over us (2). We sense him above us, in a dominant position. His body straddles the horse, his weight solidly balanced upon its back. His arm stretches over us in the gesture of command that Michelangelo turns into the act of building. In the sixteenth century it was thought that he was Constantine, hence probably blessing. Seen as that, the effect is subtly different. But more than this— and a Greek invention—the figure assaults the place. The act, to embody the concept of human freedom, must sometimes attack or resist the environment. So one of Claes Oldenburg's first colossal projects was for a reef of concrete locked into the four corners of an intersection to block two busy streets in New York. Marcus Aurelius rides

2  Piazza del Campidoglio, equestrian figure of Marcus Aurelius, A.D. 2d century.

3

4

5

*3 Piero della Francesca, The Flagellation of Christ, ca. 1445–1450.*

*4 Caravaggio, The Calling of S. Matthew, ca. 1593.*

*5 Picasso, The Sculptor's Studio, no. 18 of the series, ca. 1930.*

forward into the void. He is not space. In these ways, through these arts, human beings learn how to be human, how to experience and to read the environment, how to shape it, and what it is like to act in it and against it, if necessary. Buildings themselves will, of course, combine the two functions in varying degrees. The more a building is expressed as a simple container of space the less sculptural it will be, but then its details may become active, then perhaps the whole massing. The Classic vernacular generally combined simple volume with sculptural details; late Modern buildings, to the detriment of the environment in urban situations, tended toward spectacularly sculptural massing. So the Farnese Palace defines its square, but also, especially in the gesture of its cornice by Michelangelo, acts sculpturally upon it, while Nôtre Dame de Ronchamp alights upon the summit of its hill like a winged victory, a sculpturally active being, gesturing to the whole horizon.

Painting works with the same human problems. If we take as example a Renaissance painting, to keep the forms more or less similar, we find Piero constructing an environment with what his generation regarded as "divine perspective" and placing in it portentous figures who are framed by it (3). They recede into its depths like frightening visions and loom forward as giants toward the frontal plane. We are moved by painting's freedom, by its power to combine act and environment in a way more intensely visionary and potentially active than can normally be achieved by architecture and sculpture. Piero's is a panel painting, free of architecture. In many cases the painting is a mural adjusted to its architectural setting, like Caravaggio's *Calling of St. Matthew* (4), where the light source in the painting, the essential element in its definition of space and action, coincides with the source of light of the chapel in which it is placed. Still, leaving such adjustments aside, we find painting evolving from Piero's use of sculptural figures in an architecturally constructed setting to Caravaggio's whole mastery of optical illusion in light. So painting, by its very nature, pursues a course aimed toward being able to create whatever it likes. But sculpture, like architecture, is not primarily illusion. It is primarily "real." It stands in real space, natural and/or man-made. To make sculpture thus resembles, recalls, or suggests an act of primitive creation. The sculptor is godlike. Dare he take on that role? Picasso shows him sleepless (5), his heavy hand on the architectural frame, the mountains of the earth far beyond, while before him his creatures, standing on a base of mountains made by him, mount each other in copulation or conflict, alive, active, and generating energy. The sculptor has created not life but something more than an image of life, certainly not a "representation" or even a "sign" of life. He has embodied life, and his creature becomes mysteriously more real than other creatures. This is the case with Picasso's goat, to which he tethers a living goat (6). The eye asks: which is real? This is sculpture's ancient aura, its magic. It is real, more real perhaps than we are. It surrounds the house. So the essence of the experience of sculpture is physical, involving an awe for life and a deep sense of physical being, a love for it, a fear of it. Sculpture is therefore essentially body. It invades space. It is not required to recreate the image of a living creature to do that. Oldenburg's *Lipstick* invaded Beinecke Plaza at Yale and confronted the columns of the Memorial there with its sad little thing hanging down (7). Like Chaplin: big space, stern authorities, poor little fellow. Hence the tracks; they suggest that it wandered in like a toy, stopped, abashed. Moved to Morse College, the *Lipstick* stood up, secure in its sympathetic entourage of closely protective towers. Not "representing" any creature, it is yet a creature; it behaves like one. Any sculpture which doesn't, and which regards its mission as primarily the modeling of space—and we shall note some of that kind later on—had better, and without prejudice regarding its quality, be called "architecture" in order to keep the operating potentialities of each art clear.

I t is a big thing to set these creatures out in the world. Each culture has approached this potent act in different ways. Egypt, as always, has the whole problem worked out so clearly and, according to its principles, so satisfyingly, that only the creatively destructive Greek mania for heroic and disruptive action was able to overthrow it. First: there are no sacred mountains in Egypt. They were made, rising over the Valley of the Nile. The pyramids at Gizeh are also sun's rays, serving the cult of Ra, like the pyramidia of his obelisks, as if the shafts were buried in the ground. They create a new environment, changing this world, harnessing the sun, making everything all right forever. So their Pharaohs sit in the Valley temples below them in complete confidence. They seek the immobility of the block of stone out of which just enough is carved away to reveal them sitting there. Their eyes are open forever; the hawk of Egypt, the unwinking bird, directs their eyes, like those of the Sphinx above them, toward the sun. They are transfixed by its rays. So, in this case, they are alive forever precisely because, though minimally articulated for movement, they do not move. They do not wink in the sun. So they as bodies are always ready, literally, to house the Pharaoh and to fix him in the eternal life of his god, the sun.

Equally in standing statues (8). Potentially active, they choose not to act but instead to assume their timeless, ritual roles: sister-wife who supports husband-brother Pharaoh, his headdress flat-planed, sharp-edged, and aggressive, hers soft-contoured and rounded, her body a stalk, his a trunk rising in a broad V, while his legs subside downward from the knee in enormously heavy masses, the whole compression of his weighty body

6

7

6  *Picasso*, Goat, *1950. With real goat outside Picasso's villa.*

7  *Claes Oldenburg*, Lipstick *(first version), Yale University, 1969.*

8

8　*Mycerinus and his Queen, Egypt, 3d millennium B.C.*

9　*Courtyard, Palace at Knossos, Crete, 2d millennium B.C.*

10　*Flank and eastern hill, Second Temple of Hera, Paestum, ca. 450 B.C.*

11　*West front, Second Temple of Hera.*

flowing downward into great feet spreading out on the earth. She embraces the trunk like a vine. The empathetic experiences and the associational references are infinitely rich in what may at first seem to be very simple forms.

If the Egyptians had the problems of human life worked out in a way that encouraged the embodiment of life in monumental immobility, the Bronze Age Minoans did not. Their sacred mountains were natural ones like Mount Jouctas, seen down the length of the court of the royal palace at Knossos (9). The man-made form is a longitudinally extended hollow, sited so as to receive the sculptural force of the mountain, whose horns came charging down the court when the bull dance took place within it. The dancers seized those horns and let themselves be launched into space when the bull tossed his head. That act embraced nature's power and was shaped by it exactly as the court itself was. Action was everything but was generated by nature's energy; it did not oppose nature's force. It is probably for those reasons that Minoan civilization does not seem to have produced monumental sculpture. The permanent immobility of Egypt was of no use to this cult, wherein the fluid movements of the dance as a whole could most easily be embodied in groupings of small bronze, terra-cotta, or ivory figurines. At the same time, nature was all; she was not challenged; so no counter force, either architectural or sculptural, was brought to bear to balance her forms.

It was the Greeks who did this (10). The Greek temple stands up as a clearly man-made form, shaped to confront the sacred landscape. Inside, it houses the image of its divinity. Outside, it makes the character of that being physically manifest in empathetically human terms. In this case it is Hera at Paestum, goddess who holds the land for men as their fair share, hence heavy and massive, weighing solidly on the ground, balancing the hill beyond as a man-conceived, man-made being. All previous sacred architecture, like that of Egypt, had fundamentally imitated natural forms, so calling the power of nature to themselves. Not the Greek temple. Its forms are all abstract, obviously man-imagined, but at the same time its peripteral colonnade suggests the bodies of standing human beings. It thus introduces a new element into nature: isolated man, who challenges the natural order with his own embodiments of heroic action and unquenchable desire (11). So each archaic and classic temple, before the formula dries up, is a physical body with an appropriate kind of force. Athena at Paestum is taut, vertical, and aspiring, embodying not the rich fertility of man and earth like Hera but the competitive action of the *polis* upon it. Each temple is therefore sculpture, because it is basically an active body, masking with its colonnades every indication that it contains a box of space within it. Sculpture is indeed the dominant art of the Greek archaic period. Kleobis and Biton, in myth also servants of Hera, are like

11

9

10

12 *Kleobis and Biton, Delphi, ca. 580 B.C.*

13 *Pediment relief, Temple of Artemis, Corfu, ca. 580 B.C.*

14 *Metope from Temple C, Selinus, ca. 550 B.C.*

15 *Exekias, Amphora, ca. 525 B.C. From Vulci, showing Achilles and Penthesilea.*

15

her columns, solid as oxen, bulging with compressed power (12). Their legs are articulated actively as muscular springs for action. They are athletes like the Minoan jumpers but are now tragic heros: monumental sculpture, man-sized in scale. They stand in the sacred precincts as potentially active beings, like the temple. It is all one art.

The bodies of the temples also support figural sculpture. From the earliest period these figures were used as an enhancement of the temple's own physical power. At Corcyra the Gorgon crowned the pediment, culminating the building's force and projecting it menacingly outward (13). Therefore she and her attendant offspring and guardian felines are cut as fully in the round as possible. They are almost entirely freestanding, unlike Egyptian architectural relief which repeated the plane of the wall or floated within it. Egyptian "decoration," flat and bright whether it was painting or painted relief, thus modified its host mass by turning its planes into signs. But Greek "decoration" articulated its host body by increasing its active articulation. So the Greek figures, hotly painted, thundered with individual action on the pediment, roughly adjusted to its shape but at first without any dramatic unity among themselves. In the metopes it was the same (14). Here the heros stood forth, quintessential figural concentrations of the temple's own heroic stance. Hercules, subduing nature's monsters, was always foremost among them.

In these ways the Greek temple, which was the foundation of the Western tradition of collaboration between the arts, was in fact the result of the dominance of one art, sculpture, and of an extraordinarily powerful and single-minded view of the sacred building as a single body, the intrinsically unified embodiment of aggressive sculptural power. For these reasons, archaic painting is sculptural as well. Most of it which remains is on vases. They, too, are actively physical forms, bursting with hearty life (15). Their taut geometry, as in all Greek art, is used to firm up the activity of the form. They are of the same family as the columns and the kouroi, and the figures painted on them are like the sculpture in the pediments and metopes. They are solid, defined by clear lines and planes, not shadowed by atmosphere but carved out of the black pigment or built up in red and white paint. They are isolated and heroic too, neither environmental nor spatial. Upon the swelling chests of the vases the male heros smite their enemies, monster or Amazon. All this of course was entirely the opposite of what painting was to become when it freed itself from sculpture's "reality" and discovered its own gift for illusion. The shift to the red figure style in Greek vases was the first step in that process. The figure was no longer engraved but drawn with a pen or a brush on the natural surface of the vase and now gave off light against the polished black pigment around it, leaping forward off the surface, where before if most of the vase was to be made black, a metope frame had to be cut for its own black body to stand out against the terra-cotta ground. Then, with Polygnotus and the other great painters of the fifth century, painting became monumental, intellectually and emotionally complicated and expressive, achieving tragic stature and undoubtedly affecting sculpture, as in the pediments of the new Temple of Zeus at Olympia. The figures are now fitted into their frame like paintings and are clearly meant to be seen from below with an adjustment to perspective angle. Most of all, they now embody not only physical being but also states of mind, reflecting the individual soul, by stance and expression, in exactly the way for which Polygnotus was famous. The great *Iliupersis* of Polygnotus at Delphi was conjecturally restored by Robert in 1893 from Pausanias's extensive description of it in the second century A.D. (16). Looking at its major themes, the horse rolling over, the dead warrior, the seated figures with children in their arms, the great beast that overlooks the scene, we cannot fail to observe that all the figures of Picasso's *Guernica* of 1937 are to be found there (17). It was clearly Picasso's primary model—a fact which has inexplicably escaped comment by his historians—a model reformed into pedimental shape and fused into violent action by another contemporary work of Greek art, the west pediment at Olympia (18). The draped arm of the central figure there, whether Apollo or Peirithous, is even echoed in the arm of Picasso's woman rushing in from our right toward the center of the *Guernica*. So Greek painting's first moment of monumental dominance eventually affected the creation of one of painting's foremost monuments in the twentieth century. What Greek painting itself accomplished is reflected for us at some remove by Roman frescoes, like those from Boscoreale in the Metropolitan Museum of Art (19, 20). A convincing and realistic perspective is created, based on the fact that we focus only on one percent of the space directly before us but are optically aware of everything within a full 180° arc of vision (20). The Greco-Roman painter thus wraps a wide wall around us or, in smaller, more vertical spaces, will lead us on a walk, looking down at a garden bench, up at a pergola (19). He will sometimes cut, by illusion, what seem to be small windows in his walls, to show us an extensive landscape, often seen from above and far off. In such landscapes he paints those sacred features which had originally been worshiped at their full scale, and as he brings them into the optical illusion of a perspective system he dematerializes architecture into an optical play of light as well (21). He now creates the whole environment and endows it with a nostalgic, Theocritean glow.

Some of the old awe is past; nature itself is being shaped. Hence architecture too becomes environmental; the temple loses a good deal of its old muscular bulk, while its attendant propylaia

16

17

18

19

20                                 21

16  Polygnotus, Iliupersis, ca. 475 B.C. Conjectural reconstruction by Robert, 1893.

17  Picasso, Guernica, 1937.

18  West pediment sculptures, Temple of Zeus, Olympia, ca. 460 B.C.

19  Wall paintings of corner of room from villa at Boscoreale, A.D. 1st century.

20  Wall paintings from villa at Boscoreale, A.D. 1st century.

21  Sacred Landscape, wall painting from Pompeii, A.D. 1st century.

22 Acropolis at Lindos, Rhodes, 4th–2d centuries B.C. Conjectural reconstruction of model, from the north, 1960.

23 Detail, Empress Theodora, mosaic in San Vitale, Ravenna, A.D. early 6th century.

24 Left wall of apse, showing mosaic of Justinian and his attendants, San Vitale, Ravenna, A.D. early 6th century.

25 Interior (from a watercolor), Hagia Sophia, Istanbul, A.D. 6th century.

26 Nave, Church of La Madeleine, Vezelay, 12th century.

27 Capital showing temptation of S. Anthony, Church of La Madeleine, Vezelay.

and stoas open out into enclosing, space-making frames of slender columns (22). The architect even touches up, like a painter, the sacred landscape features to make them more conical, more optically appropriate. This is the illusionistic world of the Hellenistic and Imperial periods. But it transforms itself into the Christian Middle Ages by turning its optical gifts to a new transcendent focus, not on the sun-struck shapes of this world but on the hypnotic dazzle of the next (23). Mosaic, an ancient art, now especially serves these desires and rivets our attention on the splendors of a heavenly light. It replaces sculpture, climbs up on the walls and adjusts itself to their curvature, shaping an environment of weightless splendor and hieratic dreams (24). "Decoration," to touch again on that theme, dematerializes the architectural plane. This all culminates in Hagia Sophia, where, unlike the Parthenon (but the same divinity, Wisdom, directs both programs), the point of the building is not to blaze as a victorious sculptural body in the landscape under the light of day, but to create a vast interior environment within which human beings can find psychic shelter (25). All pressures and weights are transcended in the dazzle of the mosaic and in the magically floating canopy of the golden dome, heaven's symbol. The exterior of Hagia Sophia is simply a shell to contain this space; it makes a great bridge to heaven, surmounted by the dome, but it is not itself solidly figural, like the temple, but hollow, thus environmental, in its effect. For all these reasons figural sculpture, that so intensely pagan, bodily art, progressively dwindles away in this transcendent pictorial environment, eventually to come under actual iconoclastic prohibition for a considerable length of time.

Where and how does monumental figural sculpture come back? It does so in Romanesque Western Europe and in ways which suggest that it was generated by the architectural environment itself. The Romanesque church is as much a dominant environmental shelter as Hagia Sophia, but, though painted, it is not weightless but solidly structural and massive (26). Its small windows are cut deeply into heavy walls, whose weight is carried by compound piers which are profoundly sculptural, almost figural, ponderously deploying their masses outward from their thick inner blocks to fat, round colonnettes resting heavily upon the pavement. Right at the capitals, where the structure's dramatic transferral of weight can be most felt, there the figural sculpture appears, men and monsters squirming into active life as if generated by the compressive heat of the stone (27). The figures are thus primarily an outgrowth of the environment and conform to its architectural shape. As decoration, they bring the mass to life. They do not challenge it. They don't even really populate it; they are of it. Elsewhere, over doorways, where the structural facts of the environment require only a thin slab of stone, because the weight is being taken by the arch above it, the figures again appear. (28). Now, though, they are flattened laterally to conform to the character of that thin plane. They burn with excited linear fires and offer up their emotion to the environment, scorching along the surface of the stone.

One of the very first things that the architecture which can be identified as Gothic did was to pull those figures forward from their plane into a solid three dimensions (29). Instantly, as at Chartres, they became grave and calm, belonging in the environment but not dominated by it—creating a truce, a peace. Down below, the figures turn into statue columns, vertical and stiff, wholly obeying the architecture's law but again forward of its plane and sweet-faced in human contentment and dignity. Now they are a self-respecting population, a delegation of gentle beings sent to greet us on arrival. Inside they all disappear in a new kind of transcendent light, grander and more mysterious, more purely come from heaven even than that reflected off the mosaics of the East (30). It is the light of stained glass, for which in large measure the whole Gothic edifice was raised. In it figures swim like droplets of color, their narrative function subordinate to the overall, environmental color screen. Soon they become larger and the glass clearer; they begin to exercise their power as figures upon the environment. An early example of that is the famous Virgin of the Belle Verrière who comes floating in with the sun in the south ambulatory of the choir at Chartres (31). She is a creature of light, and as she is seen from the crossing under the arches of the transept, she balances the Black Virgin who holds the dark north ambulatory, seen at exactly the same angle on the other side, from the same climatic point in front of the choir. Down below in the crypt sits the Vierge sous Terre, the third of the triad.

It is out of the light of the Belle Verrière that the late medieval painting of northern Europe essentially derives (32). Van Eyck's droplets of oil capture the light within them. The solid physical body which Italian painters like Giotto had achieved a hundred years before is turned magical by this interior light. The perspective is hypnotic, magical itself. Van Eyck seems perfectly clear about this: he brings the Virgin as a giant down from the now wholly clear glass windows and has her fill the vessel of the church—illusionistically, as only painting could achieve it. He shows us the mystery of the Mass, ultimate sacrifice of the Lamb (33), and he makes us grasp it visually with methods which recall those of Greece and Rome (20). We focus on the critical, bright spot in the center, while out around it, as White has shown, swells a barrel of figures exactly shaped to fill the oval frame of our vision. We take in the whole without strain, on a ground plane tipped up to contain and to let us perceive it all, including great cities in the distance, as magically clear as the flowers in the grass before us.

28

29

30

31

33

32

28 Center portal of the narthex, Church of La Madeleine, Vezelay.

29 West portals, Cathedral of Chartres, ca. 1145–1150.

30 Nave, Chartres, ca. 1200.

31 "La Belle Verriere," stained glass window in the south ambulatory, Chartres, ca. 1200.

32 Jan van Eyck, Madonna in a Church, ca. 1425.

33 Jan and Hubert van Eyck, "The Adoration of the Lamb," center panel, The Ghent Altarpiece, 1432.

We see it all, but we are not in it; it is indeed a visionary world. What the Italian Renaissance does above all is to pull us into the painting space, to make us walk into it and among its noble sculptural figures, set like columns at our eye level, standing on the same ground plane as we (34). As they deploy back into space, the landscape that marches with them becomes misty in a perspective illusion now atmospheric as well as linear. Perhaps for the first time in painting (since we do not really know what all the lost Greeks did) a relation between figure and landscape is set up which is as solid and physically persuasive as that achieved by the Greek temple in its landscape. A new heroic confrontation is thus achieved. But that relationship is, by definition, not an easy one. It is hard to set the heroic act free and still have it fit into an environment. There is a strong contradiction in modes of being involved. Pollaiuolo shows us that the optics are demanding (35). The viewer must look left and right to take it all in—unlike Van Eyck's focus which holds us steady—while the figures seem to loom over the landscape behind them. The difficulty is not so much technical as conceptual. How can the free act, which the Greeks opposed in a tragic balance with the environment, be made to fit into it? Fate and free will, how reconciled? This was an especially difficult question because the Renaissance was above all the freeing of European man to act on his own without the old environment to sustain him. Its very first sculpture shows this. That is, the Gothic statue column had slowly gained the power to act—to move, group, and converse—but only within and respecting the frame of architectural environment. The whole beautiful development from Reims to Sluter shows this. The final achievement is dramatic, not revolutionary. But a contrast between St. Theodore on the south porch of Chartres and Donatello's St. George in his shallow niche at Or San Michele shows the change (36, 37). St. Theodore, though he carries his weight on his own feet, is bound up with the environment, supported and canopied by it. The twist of the column below him is continued by his baldric to bind him into place. His strength is in his faith, his submission. Donatello's St. George is alone, pushed forward out of his shallow niche. He is nervous, taut, and aggressive, a creature of will and anxiety, already a modern man, liberated from the environment and from trust in it, free and alone to act as he can in the world. This is why the Renaissance begins (if we may employ such a term) precisely with sculpture, indeed with those figures by Donatello of the first two decades of the fifteenth century. It begins with the act.

A new environment soon follows. Brunelleschi, disappointed sculptor, creates it (38). It is based on the new perspective, which Manetti tells us that Brunelleschi invented, and upon the Vitruvian figure, undoubtedly reflecting Pythagorean and perhaps Platonic idealism, of the

34

35

36

37

38

34  Masaccio, The Tribute Money, *fresco from the Brancacci Chapel in S. Maria del Carmine, Florence, ca. 1425–1427.*

35  Antonio Pollaiuolo, Rape of Deianira, *ca. 1470.*

36  *Jamb statues from the South Porch, Chartres, ca. 1200.*

37  Donatello, S. George, *ca. 1415–1417. Bronze copy in place on Or San Michele, Florence.*

38  Filippo Brunelleschi, *loggia, Ospedale degli Innocenti, Florence, 1419–1421.*

man of perfect proportions who fits into the primary shapes of the universe, the circle and the square (39). Brunelleschi's architecture is like Leonardo's drawing of that figure. The environmental shapes of circle and square, of cube and sphere, are spatial, not sculptural. They are drawn tight as wire, stretched into thin frames and canopies by the overwhelming desire to make space, not mass. The observer, the human being, is the active sculptural figure; the architecture is pure, perfect volumes of space. But this system of space making is so exact and complete that there is no place for sculpture in it, and not much really for painting either (40). Here an intense conflict is apparent, between the idea of liberated action in sculpture and of the perfect environment in architecture. How can they be brought together? Ideally, only in painting, where the sculptural figures can be fitted through illusion into the perspective box (41). Here the West settles, and has continued to do so since that time, for free investigation rather than for contentment, for an imagined future rather than present ease. In this way the magnificent dominance of Renaissance painting over the other arts begins to take shape. In the largest sense it continues right up to the present day. The conjunction of environment and act is made only with enormous tension and difficulty, as we have already noted, so that it remains an engrossing, profoundly intellectual and emotional problem (3), endowing Baroque and Modern painting with that quality of inexhaustibility and discovery which it may only be at the very edge of losing right now. But so far as sculpture is concerned, there is clearly no place for it in the new Renaissance scheme of things. There is really no place for it on church facades, where concern is for an expression of the perfect harmony of circle and square. San Lorenzo never gets a facade, thus remaining a purely spatial perspective box. Michelangelo projected one for it: circles and squares. The first concerted project for a new Renaissance church exterior was in fact Alberti's for Rimini—circle, cube, and sphere, at once purely conceptual and heavy with Roman gravity (42). All the solids were in a sense a decoration; they brought drawing into mass. Palladio perfected the type (43). Sculpture, where present, is so placed and confined as to seem purposefully inhibited and repressed.

If so, what of the act? Michelangelo poses that question early in his career. The *David* is a giant ready for action (44). The hand swells with the immanence of the cast stone; the profile is determined. The whole young body is trained down, lean and hard. It is ready. But then, as so many observers have noted, when we move to the side everything changes. The body becomes a pliant stalk without force, supporting a head too large for it (45). The face expresses doubt, perhaps fear, perhaps sympathy. There is in any event uneasiness about the character of action, a sense, guilt-ridden and very non-Greek, of action's

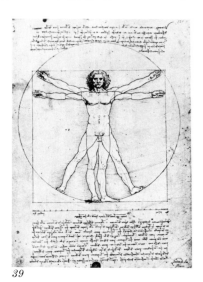
39

41

40

43

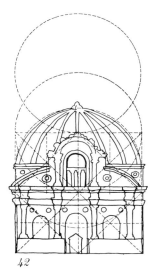
42

39  Leonardo da Vinci, Vitruvian "Man of Perfect Proportions," ca. 1500.

40  Filippo Brunelleschi, interior, S. Lorenzo, Florence, 1425.

41  Masaccio, Trinity, fresco, S. Maria Novella, Florence, ca. 1425.

42  Leon Battista Alberti, S. Francesco, Rimini, ca. 1445–1450. Theoretical analysis of facade by C. Ragghianti.

43  Andrea Palladio, Il Redentore, Venice, 1577–1592.

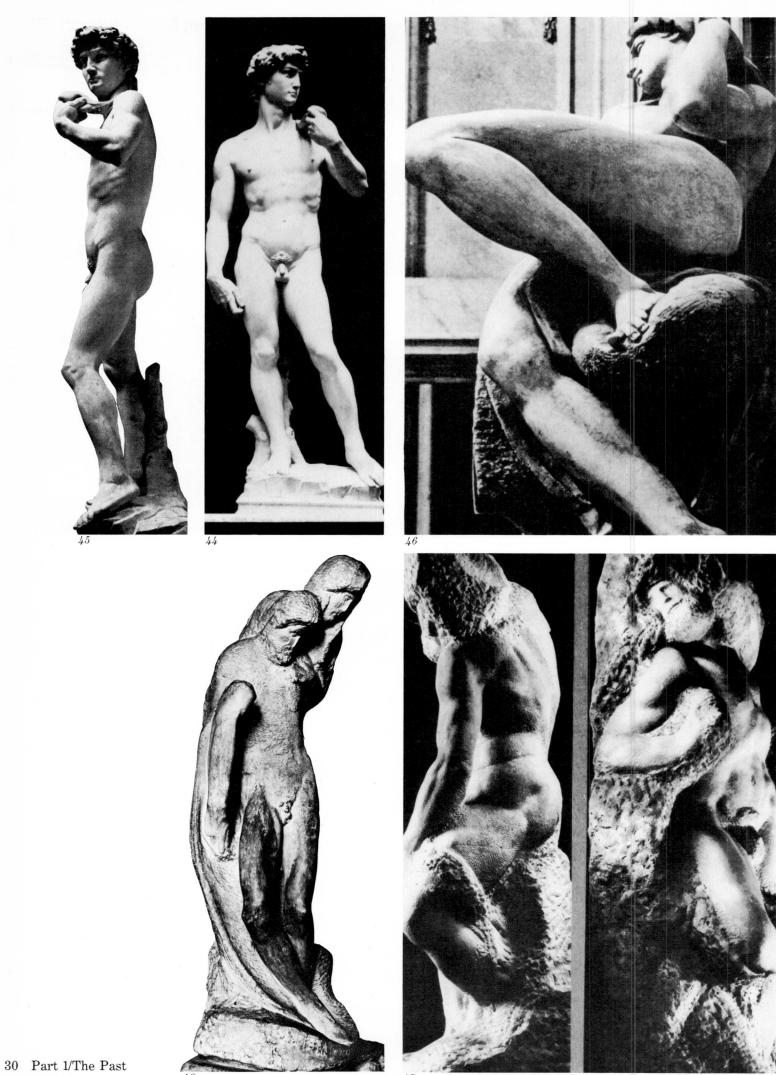

45

44

46

48

47

ambiguous justifications. Is action worthwhile? This means: is it worthwhile making sculpture? Michelangelo's enormous compassion wars with his superhuman vitality over this ambiguity all his life. The struggle itself endows his sculpture with its special life-in-depth, far beyond anything Greek, and with its eternal restlessness (46). Physical, passionate, yearning in and through the flesh, it is also rent with soul, with abnegation and sorrow. Is it worthwhile to emerge from the stone (47)? So much pain. Is it worth it to be born? Finally, at the very end of his life, indeed as he is dying, Michelangelo seems to say, no, it is not worth it— to sink back into the arms of the mother is all. With his last strength he lops off the heroic arm and shoulder of the Christ in the Rondanini Pietà (48), and as the forms fall back and subside, he scrapes—one can feel his life waning—scratches with his clawed chisel on the surface of the stone, roughening the forms, turning the faces back into formlessness and decay, like Monet's painted veil across his dead wife's face. But as the shapes fall back they assume a prehistoric form; a carved tusk, like an ivory, and this, gathering itself, arches up and over like a wave about to break, the arc rising as Michelangelo dies, so left at the edge of its ultimate action forever.

In the end, Renaissance sculpture can thus be said to disappear at the hands of its greatest sculptor, because of the paradox that action poses for the thinking mind. The act cannot challenge the environment forever. Eventually it merges with it. This is exactly what it does in Baroque architecture and sculpture. Just as Baroque painting conquers illusion wholly and thus controls a total environment, so Baroque architecture and sculpture merge into a pictorial drama. It is modeled in light like painting and is framed and directed as upon a stage. Bernini's Cornaro Chapel is all that (49). The donors watch from the box, like Rembrandt's syndics attending (50), while the play goes on. St. Theresa's ecstasy, spot-lit, is echoed in the pediment above her which bursts open with release. The facade of Borromini's San Andrea alle Quattro Fontane justifies its name by environmentally controlling the crossing of its streets, while the gestures of the figures in its niches seem to direct the undulations of its facade and to project them upward to the culminating painted oval in the center (51). Contrast should be made with Palladio's Redentore, where the gestures of the sculptural figures, active enough in themselves, are squelched by the tight niches and sat on by the heavy pediments above them (43). At San Carlo the niches open up, the pediment breaks, the environment consents to the act so that in fact there is no confrontation between these two opposites any more but only a rhythmic oneness, the famous Baroque principle of unity at work. But that very union robs the act of its intensity. The heavy price that is paid for it, therefore, is the loss of sculpture's special, primitive aura, in which it

49

50

51

44  *Michelangelo*, David, *1503.*

45  *Michelangelo, side view,* David, *1503.*

46  *Michelangelo, figure of Dawn,* Tomb of Lorenzo de Medici, *ca. 1525.*

47  *Michelangelo,* Captives, *ca. 1532.*

48  *Michelangelo,* The Rondanini Pietà, *1564.*

49  *Bernini, the Cornaro Chapel in S. Maria della Vittoria, Rome, 1644–1652.*

50  *Rembrandt van Rijn,* The Syndics of the Cloth Guild, *1661.*

51  *Francesco Borromini, lower section of facade, S. Carlo alle Quattro Fontane, Rome, 1665–1667.*

52

53

54

55

56

57

52  *Piazza Navona, Rome, 17th century.*

53  *Louis Le Vau, Château and gardens of Vaux-le-Vicomte, 1656–1661.*

54  *John Constable,* Salisbury Cathedral, *1826.*

55  Columbia, *World's Columbian Exposition, Chicago, 1893.*

56  Landscape, *fresco painting from Pompeii, A.D. 1st century.*

57  *Claude Monet,* Woman under the Trees in a Meadow, *1881.*

invades the environment, may threaten it or us, may be somehow dangerous and therefore peculiarly alive. Now we know that it is theater and so not ultimately serious—and marvelous theater, like that back and forth play, eventually illuminated at night, between sculpture and architecture in the Piazza Navona (52). Here the Italian seventeenth century's greatest architect and sculptor come together and thus demonstrate the Baroque's special strength in architecture and sculpture as well as its severest limitations. It is play, in which sculpture, though endlessly delightful, in fact merges into the environment and its special dangerous presence is lost. In that sense, decoration is all.

This again is the reason why painting—with the exception of a couple of generations which are dominated by the French classic garden—remains the dominant art. Only Vaux, Versailles, and Chantilly can so merge the act into a total architectural environment (53). Painting's dominance, which may be said to have created the English landscape garden itself, finally culminates in the nineteenth century (54). So Constable can lead us into his world and can merge us with it precisely because painting has now become the wholly environmental art into which the act can be inextricably woven. Sculpture, on the other hand, tends, despite its various neoclassic reactions, to become increasingly pictorial right up to the later years of the nineteenth century, and it is no accident that it was the Baroque world of dramatic unity which was revived at Chicago in 1893 (55). The old synthesis still held because the sculpture was still eminently, indeed increasingly, pictorial, the figures disembodied into brushstrokes of light and dissolving into the background like those in the illusionistic frescoes of Rome (56). That development was also sociologically exact, since it was the fundamental objective of the nineteenth-century middle class—and had indeed been a Roman objective as well—to discourage anarchic acts and to create a safe, integrated environment. This is the environment into which we are optically drawn by the greatest painter of the age, Monet, as he merges figures and places into one veil of color, unifying all (57). It is the very height of painting's capacity to draw us into the magical spaces of dreams. Looking into the little ponds with their water lilies and finding the whole sky reflected in them, we sink into the depths and into the clouds as well.

At a fundamental level, this merger with nature may be said to have been the most advanced state of the arts around 1890. It was in accord with nineteenth-century scientism and with its belief in continuous process, and its most obvious architectural union occurred in Art Nouveau and, even more splendidly, in the related work of Antoni Gaudi. The academic reaction of the nineties can be regarded as having been directed in large part against that very merger. It has always been the academic's intention to have things clear and categorized, and a thinned-out and rationalized classicizing form has, over the past several centuries, generally served as the academic language of the visual arts. It was founded on the Baroque synthesis but shared little of the Italian Baroque's intensity. Its background was primarily French and was ultimately grounded in the classicism of Poussin. That tradition had indeed been kept functional by the pedagogic continuity of the French Academy. There can be no doubt that with the nineteenth-century reorganization of the Beaux-Arts some clear thinking took place about the relationship between the arts and—again the archetypal Beaux-Arts program—their collaboration in the shaping of the environment. This seems especially true in America, perhaps because the concept of a new Renaissance was so consciously and enthusiastically embraced here. It had, moreover, a splendid beginning: with Richardson and La Farge at Trinity Church in Boston, where the forms were by no means classical and the achievement was far more than academic. The whole interior is one warm glow— what Hitchcock called a "mist" of living color—to which the great western stained glass windows by La Farge contribute the noblest share and set a grand scale of united tone. La Farge's figural panels around the church, in which he was assisted by Saint-Gaudens, are of a similar gentle grandeur. One feels that the best of the century is here. As was soon to be the case in Chicago, the environment is indeed all; the vast colored volume of space is deeply pictorial, but the ambient is firm and monumental. A sculptural solemnity, in that sense truly Romanesque, and absent in Chicago, shapes the whole.

Out of this beginning, by the 1890s, came other achievements in collaboration by architects who had in part been trained by Richardson. None was of his pure genius, but, like him, they were all imbued with the academic system and knew how to employ it. So McKim, Mead, & White set up their Boston Public Library on Copley Square across from Trinity in the rational manner of Labrouste at the Bibliothèque Ste. Geneviève, though they cannot help softening and archaeologizing his taut, spare forms. But like him they lead us through the ground floor to a stair that rises at the rear of the building to attain the main reading rooms of the upper floor. Where Labrouste used a copy of Raphael's *School of Athens* on the rear wall, McKim, Mead, & White open theirs more widely to light and direct us upward to the climax in enlightenment by means of the murals of Puvis de Chavannes (58). These are classicizing and, like the building, not the most intense of forms, but they are dynamically adjusted to the architectural frame and so flow up the stairs and float toward the empyrean of the top landing (59).

That association of basically classical academic figures with essentially classical academic architecture went on to produce some of fresco

59

58

58 *McKim, Mead, & White, main staircase, Boston Public Library, 1888–1892.*

59 *Puvis de Chavannes, murals, Boston Public Library, 1892.*

60

61

60 Diego Rivera, murals on the principal stairway of the National Palace, Mexico City, 1929–1930.

61 Orozco, painted dome from the auditorium of the University of Guadalajara, Mexico, 1929.

painting's greatest triumphs in the twentieth century. The system was able to transform the airy fantasies of Puvis de Chavannes into the tumultuous proletarian crowds of Diego Rivera, whose revolutionary figures boil out of the walls along the stairway and around the courtyard of Mexico's National Palace (60). They do not fit into the architecture but swamp it; they occupy the government building like a revolutionary army. The whole vast achievement of the Mexican collaboration among the arts was possible because it had this program. It was aimed toward a revolutionary end; it was trying to arouse, teach, and triumph. Giotto returns, since now a story must be told movingly and clearly, and the broad, blunt figures, endlessly eloquent in their gestures, can be turned to a Mexican purpose with Aztec sculptural power. Orozco is different; his forms attack the environment with fire and reform it in their flames (61). He and Rivera are thus poles apart, and this itself shows the vitality of their common tradition, since they were after all working in an old and disciplined mural system which they were able to infuse with the bite of new objectives and beliefs. During that curious period of the recent past when the stylistic movement toward abstraction was considered more significant than matters of quality and meaning, or was regarded as synonymous with them, the Mexican muralists were generally undervalued, though not, it must be noted, in Mexico. It should now be obvious that they were giants, their quality absolute; they blew an old world apart with their uniquely pictorial union of sculptural and environmental aggression.

The painters of the American scene who painted murals under the auspices of various public agencies during the thirties were directly inspired to a mural art by the example of the Mexicans, as was the decision of the New Deal administration to commission them. But with the exception of Shahn who painted as a pure Social Democrat at Roosevelt, New Jersey, and elsewhere, they were generally less certain than the Mexicans about what the social meanings and objectives of their murals were to be. In the end, despite considerable levels of satire and of bitter social concern in their easel works, they tended in their public frescoes to construct a hymn of praise for the continent, especially for the Middle West, and for the human beings, larger than life, who framed it or had shaped its history. So their murals, though heroic in intention, tended also to be elegiac or descriptive. Hence they were never as aggressive as those of the Mexicans: they did not attack the environment but eulogized it and so never achieved the power that could blast old frameworks and suggest new ones. They are weaker than the Mexicans but have also been seriously undervalued nonetheless. Benton is splendidly resourceful in space and incident at Indiana University and the Missouri State Capitol, Curry epic in Topeka; while Grant Wood, whom even the most recent student of the American scene characterizes as not a very good painter, is in fact the gravest and noblest of them all when seen on the broad stretches of wall which he respects so intensely or in his studies for them. He is not Giottoesque like Rivera but of the Quattrocento, recalling Piero and Uccello. His figures are sculpturally conceived, enthroned in clear stages of space.

Traditional sculptural character was therefore a primary ingredient in the most effective of all the figural mural series from the 1890s to 1940. (We saw earlier that much the same was true of the *Guernica* of 1937.) What of sculpture itself and its relation to architecture during those years? At first, as in Chicago, it retained its power to act effectively, though in the continuing neo-Baroque accord with the environment. For example, Grand Central Station by Reed & Stem and Warren & Wetmore embodied the rush of the trains below it and of the automobile traffic around it by setting off Mercury's rush forward against the point marker of the New York Central office tower far back across the open space. The sense of flight and freedom is compelling—or was so until Pan Am (much maligned surely, but deservedly so) brutally blocked the view.

Everywhere during the generation of the 1880s to about 1910, sculptors like Saint-Gaudens knew how to populate the environment and to bring it alive with their embodiments of action. Farragut steams forward against the current, damning the torpedoes in Central Park. We empathetically stand with him; by association we share his danger. Sherman on horseback comes clip-clopping down Park Avenue, sawing on the reins, head bare, brow bent back as with one of his migraines, the fruit of awareness (62). Victory strides before him. He rides like War, Famine, Pestilence, and Death behind her. Most of all, Colonel Shaw marches with his black troops down Beacon Street (63). It is all there as Robert Lowell said it in his ode "For the Union Dead":

Their monument sticks like a fishbone
in the city's throat.
Its Colonel is as lean
as a compass needle.

He has an angry wrenlike vigilance,
a greyhound's gentle tautness;
he seems to wince at pleasure,
and suffocate for privacy.
. . . . .
when he leads his black soldiers to death,
he cannot bend his back.

It is probably to be expected that the most desperate experience in American history before 1917, the Civil War, should have triggered its most consistent and significant sculptural response. At the head of the Mall in Washington, Grant, motionless in the saddle, guards the Capitol; its

62

63

62  *Augustus Saint-Gaudens, Sherman Monument, Central Park Plaza, New York, 1903.*

63  *Augustus Saint-Gaudens, Shaw Memorial, Boston Common, 1897.*

64

65

66

64  Interior, Lincoln Memorial, with statue by Daniel Chester French, Washington, D.C., 1912–1922.

65  Air view, Lincoln Memorial.

66  View from Lincoln Memorial statue towards Washington Monument.

dome, under construction all through the war, rises behind him. He stares down the long vista toward the Potomac, still as an animal, dangerous as Hell, his slouch hat pulled over his eyes. To left and right field artillery is coming to his support, the horses reeling, the guns bouncing behind them. Down the long axis, far off, his back to the Potomac, America's major cult figures broods, as real a presence to us as Zeus was to Phidias at Olympia (64). Like that Zeus he is set back in the shadows of a temple's cella, illuminated only through the open door and by whatever artificial light (cressets perhaps then, an electric bulb now—it doesn't make any difference) seemed necessary to reveal his being. But to terminate the axis more firmly, this temple is turned so as to present its broad side to the Mall (65), and through it Lincoln looks out toward the obelisk of the Washington Monument (66) and, in the far distance, toward his necessary instrument, the great general in front of the dome. How large a part association plays in the experience of public monuments can be tested in people of my generation by recalling our reaction to these forms before and after the Kennedy funerals. It is true that a change in critical stance has also occurred over that period. We now appreciate classicizing academic art as once we did not. But much more than that is the overlay of images which have soaked these monuments in blood and sorrow: John Kennedy's noble caisson passing around the Lincoln Memorial in solemn cortege and crossing the bridge to Arlington, and there, finally and unbearably, the flag taken off the coffin and folded in neat quick folds and placed in the widow's hands. Even more: Robert Kennedy's funeral, when the train with his body, delayed after tragic accidents along the line from New York, sent the hearse late to the Lincoln Memorial in darkness and rain, while those from the Poor People's encampment, who had waited for it all day, stretched out their hands toward it in front of the colonnade with the image behind them until the hearse picked up speed and moved away to show us at last on our television screens, not the Irish Guards in formation as at John's interment, but the open grave in the rain and the dead man's son, the first of the pallbearers, staggering up the slope toward it, his face twisted in unspeakable pain. Now we see the monuments of Washington, Greek and Roman as they are, in the full dimension of their cultural reference and can say with them, "The Gracchi are dead, Tribunes of the people. Now comes night." And the night came.

What happened to that academic vocabulary of forms, that articulation of architectural frame and sculptural and pictorial presence? The answer is that it eventually lost its distinction between those parts, and the several components eventually merged into one, as the most "advanced" arts, so we noted above, had already tended to do long before. A comparison between the triumphal arch at the World's Columbian Exposition of 1893 and the main entrance to

Bertram Goodhue's Nebraska State Capitol of 1922–1927 makes that plain (67, 68). In the latter building the sculpture wholly merges with architecture and grows out of it. The mass becomes more potent, but considerable articulation (which means intellectual and emotional qualification) is lost. We are in the world of the Art Deco skyscrapers whose originally more or less classic language had been simplified, primitivized, and, from the classical point of view, barbarized over the decades. These qualities indeed shape Art Deco's power. Architecture, sculpture, and painting are all pressed back, flattened together and stripped, marvelously drawn between what were then called the Modern and the Traditional modes (69, 70). Rockefeller Center has its life in this living tension, this electric vitality; it intensifies environmental and active forces in one compressed union. Though matchless, it has its limitations, some of them perhaps conceptual. It is too bad that the lobby of the RCA Building no longer can show Rivera's mural above its elevators; it was destroyed because of its Marxist iconography. The present set is spatially spectacular but sloppy and essentially meaningless. In that vein, the lobby of the incomparable Chrysler Building is surely the most integrated, with the long ghost of the building itself riding in overhead above the entrance, while the figural sections of the ceiling coincide with the marble panels on the walls and the abstract sections with the banks of wall lights. Art Deco's jazzy conversion of old rhetorical traditions into decorative exercises—delightful but (without prejudice) superficial—thus works perfectly to celebrate the triangularity of this space with its diagonal patterns. Art Deco *is* decorative. It is not tragic drama, and while it has been deservedly revalued in recent years, it is useful to realize that this is why, in its own day, both traditionalists and pure Modernists despised it.

The "advanced" arts, of which I spoke earlier, had already primitivized themselves by the beginning of the century, but they had done so in an attempt to intensify meaning. For this reason they became sculptural rather than pictorial, casting out much of painting's power of illusion to get back to sculpture's archaic reality. So Cézanne wants his forms to seem sculpturally touchable, in contrast with Monet's optical shimmer; and Maillol (71) contrasted with MacMonnies (55) shows the difference in sculpture. Maillol's bather is structurally solid, really planted in space. Picasso picks her up, adapts her pose, merges her with African sculpture, which was, from his point of view, more primitive yet and full of the magical power that Western sculpture had given up long before (72, 73). He builds his *Demoiselles d'Avignon*, his proto-Cubist synthesis of sculpture and painting, out of these elements. The faces turn into masks. Disquieting presences begin to appear. Sculpture too takes on this quality. Lipchitz's *Figure* of 1930 has the power to project threat (74). It is not a projection of ourselves into space but a being which convinces us that it may not wish us

67

68

69

70

67  *Triumphal archway, World's Columbian Exposition, Chicago, 1893.*

68  *Bertram Goodhue, State Capitol, Lincoln, Nebraska, 1920–1926.*

69  *Raymond Hood et al., RCA Building, Rockefeller Center, New York, 1931–1939.*

70  *Main entrance, RCA Building.*

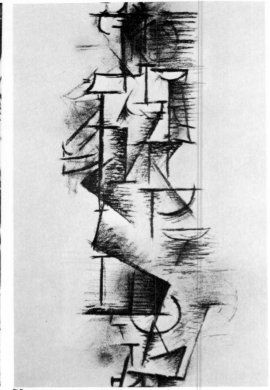

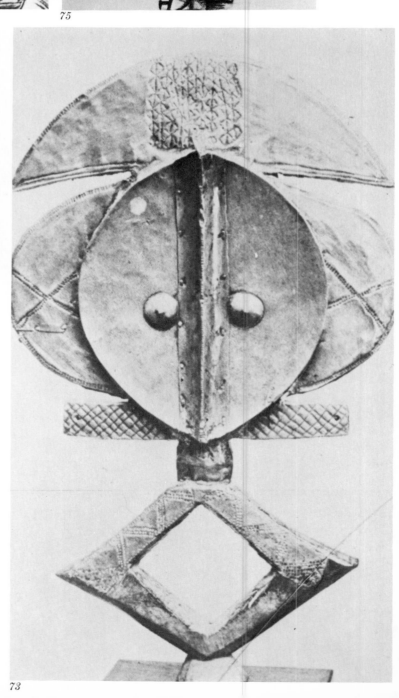

71 *Aristide Maillol*, Bather
Putting Up Her Hair, *1898.*

72 *Picasso*, Danseuse, *1907.*

73 *Nbulu-ngulu (skull-basket
guardian)*, Kuta *civilization,
Africa.*

74 *Jacques Lipchitz*, Figure,
*1929–1930.*

75 *Picasso*, Nude, *1910.*

76 *Picasso*, Artist and Model,
*illustration for* Le Chef d'Oeuvre
Inconnu *by Balzac, 1931.*

77 *Piet Mondrian, exhibition
at the Museum of Modern Art,
New York, March 1945.*

78 *Naum Gabo*, Project for a
Glass Fountain, *ca. 1925.*

79 *Calf-bearer, Acropolis,
Athens, 6th century* B.C.

80 *Picasso*, Man Carrying a
Lamb, *1944.*

well. Sculpture now regains its old aura, its menace. Cubism itself, as the *Demoiselles d'Avignon* had already suggested, was in large measure sculptural painting (75), purposefully giving up Monet's and even Cézanne's coloristic splendors in order to sweep stern vertical figures together in the center of the canvas; out of some cosmic chaos they take on body before us. Their appearance suggested several roads for sculpture and painting to travel. One of these was certainly toward abstraction. Picasso himself shows us that painting can now do anything; there are literally no boundaries to transference and illusion. His painter is not an ancient hero wrestling with living creatures, like his sculptor, but a sweaty shaved-head who draws proto-Pollocks (76) or a geometric abstraction who leaves a Greek profile on the canvas. With sculpture, existing in real space, the situation was necessarily more limited. If it became abstract but wanted to remain figurally active—in which there was no essential contradiction—the experience of it necessarily had to become more fully empathetic because it was generally less associational. One had to feel with these forms as with a structural creature, integral to itself. This is the way most of us in my generation learned to read meaning in art. An abstract sculptor, like Brancusi, might well add the associational element through a title, such as *Bird at Rest* or *Bird in Space*. The former piece of sculpture does indeed physically subside downward, and the latter does indeed physically rise and gather to leap gleamingly upward. But the names held, and their enhancement of the meaning is an indication of how empathy and association are indeed inextricably interwoven in our experience of form.

But in the movement toward abstraction some sculpture lost its figural, active quality and became environmental, thus indistinguishable from architecture and, in that definition, adding nothing to it. Abstract painting such as Mondrian's was also environmental (77). Indeed, it played a considerable part in creating the environment shaped by the International Style, in which Constructivist sculpture like Gabo's *Project for a Glass Fountain* also takes on an architectural character and loses the special sculptural stance (78). This is precisely why Picasso, the father of pictorial abstraction, never let his sculpture approach too close to that state. His figures are alive; he would be Greek if he could, but the pluralistic torment of the modern age is upon him. He loves and creates the animals, but his animal bearer, unlike its ancestor from the archaic Acropolis, must struggle to hold the beast (79, 80). The two are not locked together in a common physicality; the placid fellowship is lost. The animal is terrified; it knows that the man is a stranger in its world.

T he question of how architecture and sculpture and, secondarily, painting should relate to each other was thus raised anew by modern art. It is worthwhile to look briefly at the way the three

77

76

78

79

80

84

83

86

82

81 *Frank Lloyd Wright, interior, D. H. Martin House, Buffalo, New York, 1904.*

82 *Frank Lloyd Wright, interior, Larkin Building, Buffalo, New York, 1904. Destroyed 1950.*

83 *Frank Lloyd Wright, entrance, Susan L. Dana House, Springfield, Illinois, 1903.*

84 *Giotto, The Meeting of Joachim and Anna at the Golden Gate, fresco from the Arena Chapel, Padua, 1305–1306.*

85 *Frank Lloyd Wright, Midway Gardens, Chicago, 1914.*

86 *Frank Lloyd Wright, decorative figure, Midway Gardens, 1914.*

87 *Jackson Pollock, Blue Poles, 1953.*

major architects of the Abstract Period (as it might be called) handle that relationship. For Wright, developing out of his Froebel training as the first great architectural abstractionist, the environment was everything and all the arts were made to contribute to it. So his early houses were interwoven spatial constructions exactly scaled to their inhabitants (81). The space-defining moldings were big and insistent, crossing just above head height; they at once defined a close sense of shelter and led the eye outward to horizontally continuous space. All the furniture was scaled to the architecture. The interior was to create a perfect environment for the raising of children, disciplined, ordered, sheltering, and expansive. The effect was of great peace so long as the inhabitants accepted the environment's gentle but pervasive laws. There was no room for rebellion, therefore normally no space for sculpture. It is true that Wright loved to give his favorite clients a plaster model of the Nike of Samothrace, about four feet high (82). Hence this domesticated Victory sometimes sailed into Wright's spaces, but it hardly dominated them; instead it tended to make them look bigger by its diminished scale. Wright also sometimes employed the sculptor Richard Bock to execute pieces of sculpture that he himself had designed. Their most significant collaboration in Wright's early work (aside from the Froebel babies with their cosmic balls of yarn that crowned the piers of the Larkin Building) was in the Susan L. Dana House. There they set a penis-shaped figure, entitled *The Flower in the Crannied Wall*, directly behind the abstractly contracting and expanding entrance archway (83). The column within the female image is an ancient symbol of marriage and fertility. It occurs in those Maltese mother-goddess temples that Wright was later to recall in some of the round buildings of his last decades. Its most expressive use is by Giotto at Padua, when Joachim, learning in exile that Anna will bear a child, rushes back to Jerusalem and meets her at the Golden Gate (84). The glowing arch of the gate emits columnar forms which culminate in the cone of Joachim and Anna holding each other. The environment is literally packed with active life: an ultimate image of the objectives of the physical arts.

Wright's and Bock's most elaborate work occurred at Midway Gardens. There the columnar figures, suggestive already of Cubist influence, are totally adjusted to the architectural shapes of the environment and submissive to them (85, 86). The order is expansive and total, like an image of continental, integrated America. Everything is bound up in the stretching and interweaving of the forms, sweeping and continuous. One senses that it is in fact a uniquely American vision—to be contrasted with Giotto's contained world—of the kind in which the Abstract Expressionist painters, Jackson Pollock in particular, were later to participate, wherein all separate shapes are caught up in the swing of vast, unifying spatial rhythms (87). So Wright's work is essentially all

81

85

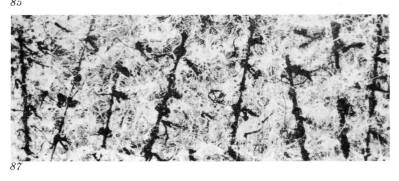

87

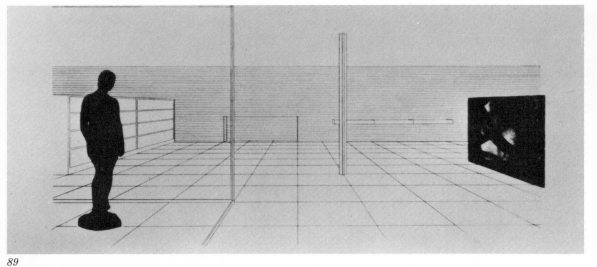

89

90

91

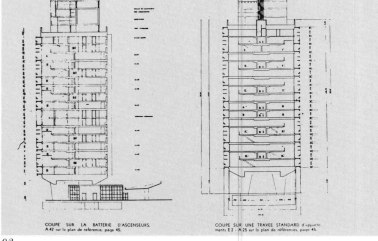

COUPE SUR LA BATTERIE D'ASCENSEURS.
A 42 sur le plan de référence, page 45.

COUPE SUR UNE TRAVEE STANDARD d'appartements E 2 - A 25 sur le plan de références, page 45.

93

88   Mies van der Rohe, German Pavilion, International Exposition, Barcelona, 1929.

89   Mies van der Rohe, interior, perspective drawing, "Court House" project, 1931–1938.

90   Mies van der Rohe, Cullinan wing, Museum of Fine Arts, Houston, Texas, 1958–1959.

91   Le Corbusier, interior, Cook House, Boulogne-sur-Seine, 1926.

92   Le Corbusier, "Le Modulor, a new human measure," 1947.

93   Le Corbusier, sections, Unite d'Habitation, Marseilles, 1948.

94   Le Corbusier, main entrance, High Court Building, Chandigarh, 1951–1956.

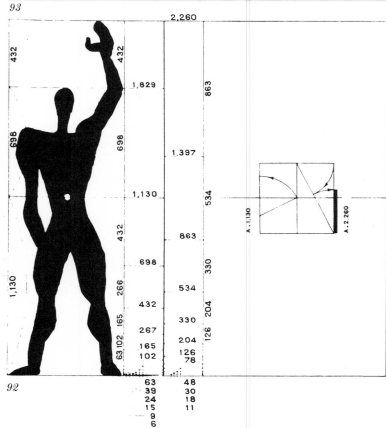

92

environment, subordinating all acts except the aura of the architect's own, and there is literally no place for painting or sculpture to operate freely within it. How could it have been otherwise in this compelling image of a nineteenth-century America determined to homogenize itself and to achieve a new, bigger, and persuasive order?

Mies van der Rohe inherits from Wright that sense of a total environment, flowing from part to part. But Mies eases off the pressure, thins out and simplifies the forms. He leads us in the Barcelona Pavilion—the cult shrine of that aspect of the Modern Movement—to a classic sculptural figure whose gesture seems to be setting the enclosing planes out in space, so creating the environment by its own act (88). In this way it recalls the Marcus Aurelius on the Campidoglio. The human act makes the world. This is why Mies would never use abstract or environmental sculpture (78) in his spaces, but instead always employed traditionally figural shapes (89). His architecture is the abstract, flowing environment, his sculpture the bodily act. Finally, in his late work, Mies settles for a less dynamic but equally grand conception, in which the solid figures are set in vast space, totally undirected and unrestrained, nobly free in a great volume of air (90). The structure, as at Houston and elsewhere, may be kept wholly outside the space in order not to intrude any compressive sense upon the liberating spatial experience. Painting, too, may hang untrammeled in those volumes, but its presence is not so keenly felt by Mies as is that of the sculpture; it is the midspace solid that he loves and the weightless planes that define the environment around it.

From the very beginning, of course, Le Corbusier's buildings were studied in pictorial and sculptural terms, which is one good reason why their appeal has been so strong and pervasive. Some of the early houses stood on legs, taut like insects but vertically stretched like people. The interior spaces were tumultuous, their shapes brought to life by rhythmically interactive elements from Le Corbusier's Purist painting itself (91). Their call is to action; they do not primarily seek to protect or to shelter a family; they are not Freudian and Oedipal like Wright's early houses, but rather *anti-Oedipe*, already schizophrenic.[1] They encourage many contradictory and rather youthfully activist modes of action, not one paternal order. In his late work Le Corbusier gathers those objectives all up into big sculptural forms. The Modular stands on its primitively muscular legs and gestures upward; so does the Unité d'Habitation at Marseilles (92, 93). So do the piers of the High Court at Chandigarh (94). Like

94

[1]Gilles Deleuze and Felix Guattari, *Anti-Oedipus: Capitalism and Schizophrenia*, trans. by Robert Hurley (New York: Viking Press, 1977). These Marxist psychiatrists seek to substitute a synthesis of Marx and Nietzsche for Freud. They dislike the family, viewing it, as Freud did, as the root of present ills but, unlike Freud, are prepared to abolish it and, in their view, to release humanity to the schizophrenia of multiple modes of behavior. Their view is independently shared by Jencks as a Post-Modern desideratum.

95

96

98

95　*Franz Kline*, Crosstown, ca. 1952.

96　*Louis I. Kahn, exhibition area, Art Gallery, Yale University, 1953.*

97　*Louis I. Kahn, fourth floor exhibition area, British Art Center, Yale University, 1972–1976.*

98　*Louis I. Kahn, Housing Government Center, Dacca, Bangladesh, ca. 1963–1966.*

97

the columns of the Temple of Athena at Paestum, they leap continuously upward with no horizontal cornice to limit their energy. Both buildings embody, in the face of a vast landscape, humanity's triumphant civic enthusiasm, what Sophocles called "the feelings that make the town."

These heroic gestures, too, seem to me to be echoed in the Abstract Expressionist painting of those same years, especially in that of Franz Kline (95). It was an Existentialist decade, which means, in art at least, an Idealistic one. Indeed, all the Abstract Period was essentially idealist, not realist, in its objectives and methods. So the three architects we have considered essentially wanted to do it all themselves and to create their own new pattern of act and environment, and they all bent reality to the shape of their overweening Idea. It is true that Wright in his own way as an American had the strongest realist component in him, while Le Corbusier was the most idealist and Mies was the closest to academic classicism. But they all set up total orders, so that the kind of collaboration between sculpture and architecture which created, for example, monumental Washington, would not have been possible under their sway. They tended to wipe out all acts other than their own or the kind they envisaged, and they permitted few associations that fell outside their system. Among them, though in widely varying degrees, in which Wright now seems much the least reductionist, they destroyed the existing architectural environment and left a pitifully reduced urbanistic language, indeed an urbanistic nightmare, in their wake.

One might infer from these unhappy developments that what was needed was to bring back an authentic academic order, perhaps the old academic system of the Beaux-Arts. That had at least belonged to a tradition which had shown itself capable of building cities and in which, as a corollary, a place had been worked out for painting and sculpture to operate fairly freely. It happens that there is one great transitional figure, Louis I. Kahn, who did in fact take the first difficult steps toward the recreation of such an order—much of which took shape, pointedly enough, in his designs for museums. Trained in the Beaux-Arts and separated from it by the dogmas of the Modern Movement, he found his way back to it, step by step and largely unconsciously, after an agonizing struggle of many years. Kahn was at the same time as idealist as his older rivals and in many ways even more abstract than they. Like them, he was convinced that he had to reinvent order from the beginning, and his first mature building, the Yale Art Gallery, does go far toward persuading us that it is a truly primitive beginning. The insistent tetrahedrons of the concrete pseudo-space frame demand to be read as a rude but inescapable law of things (96). Under them, painting and sculpture take on an intensely valuable but rather threatened life. Their very

44

being constitutes a challenge to the demanding environment which is at the same time operating according to systems, unlike those of Wright, from which it leaves them exempt. A primitively articulated academic system is thus set up. Something hard and true about the separate roles of actions and environment is being said. But finally, in his last years, as at the Kimbell Museum in Fort Worth and the British Art Center in New Haven, Kahn shapes the environment around its essential element, which is light, through which its volume and all bodies within it are wholly, gently, silently revealed (97). The effect is of permanence and peace and, in comparison with the earlier building, of a kind of death.

Again, though Kahn thought that he was beginning, he was in fact seeking out the kernel of what he had been taught in his youth: the academic, more or less classical tradition of the Beaux-Arts. So in the end it is the first of modern Beaux-Arts buildings, Labrouste's Bibliothèque Ste. Geneviève, which is his final model. His British Art Center, like Mies's buildings at IIT, is articulated fundamentally according to Labrouste's system, with a skeleton structure and in-filling panels. But Kahn's building is more physical than Mies's, more traditional, more solid in weight and mass. Kahn wanted those qualities above everything else, and he had begun to find them in the beautiful concrete planes and frames of the scholars' studies in his Salk Center, with the wooden panels set within them and with no visible sign of glass. Finally, by wrapping Roman ruins around buildings, Kahn was able to arrive at the pure voids in solid walls of Ahmedabad and Dacca (98), articulated by what he called his "brick order," that too derived from Rome. Scalelessness is sought, hence timelessness, escape from the particularities of function, permanent immobility, and, once again, the silence.

This is Kahn's final order. It is an academic classicism reduced and reconstructed at a primitive and static level. A fundamental question of this architectural generation has been how that new beginning could be carried further. Here it is interesting to observe how it has had two related but very different effects. In Europe, with Aldo Rossi and, secondarily, the other Neo-Rationalists, it was its pure solid, immobile being that was felt, and these qualities often are the foundation of Rossi's haunting work, touched, as Kahn himself was, by Di Chirico's nostalgic and disquieting spirit and by its progeny in Fascism's heavy, static, disoriented forms (99). The world is haunted by the associations they invoke, but they are being revived with new intentions, curiously innocent, linked in Rossi to the very roots of Italian tradition, in which death indeed balances life, and its city crowns the hill across from the city of the living or crowds close up to its gates. In that city are presences real but void of action. So in Rossi's cemetery projects the forms are all sculptural but wholly immobile. The silence is wholly that of

99

100

99  Aldo Rossi, architectural drawing, ca. 1975.

100  Aldo Rossi, "Teatro del Mondo," floating theater for the Venetian lagoon, 1980.

death. But in his Teatro del Mondo (100), riding its barge around the Venetian lagoon, the image is alive, like a wingless Shalako bird, high-shouldered, top-heavy, slightly goofy, and benevolent, a good-hearted clown kachina led into town.

In America, by contrast, the most important effect of Kahn's work has generally been very different from that exhibited by the Neo-Rationalists: it has been toward action rather than immobility, realism rather than idealism, irony rather than sorrow. Venturi's project for a monument in Princeton Memorial Park takes Kahn's abstract shapes at Dacca and turns them into a being, caught in a deep cry. His Guild House takes Kahn's "ruins wrapped around buildings" and transforms them into a false front on Main Street that can gesture like a sign (101, 102). The gesture is not tragic and heroic like those of Le Corbusier, but joyful, ebullient, and ironically self-deprecating. Association is invoked by calling the abstract sculpture which crowns the facade a television aerial, which it is not in fact. This special union of what seem the commonest kinds of forms (dumb and dull, Venturi calls them) with extraordinary sculptural presence in both empathetic and associational terms is an indication of where Venturi's special importance lies: he brings back traditional and vernacular architecture and endows it with contemporary communicative power. His spaces are simple; he concentrates with extraordinary humanist perception on the governing symbol, like the enormously active chimney in his famous house project of 1959. The sculptural corollary is to be found, I think, in the magically real figures of Duane Hanson, where simple, dumb, absolute imitation produces people with the terrible quality of being both alive and dead (103). They cross some line to be with us. Which is the sculptor, which the work? People who come to watch join the group. It is Pop Art's prime achievement that it has made sculpture popular. Once more, it populates.

The same is true of Venturi's Trubek and Wislocki Houses, dumb cottages as imminent as gods (104, 105). They are real, and they act. They are pure vernacular Shingle Style and lonely beings as well, standing up, turning toward each other in the fogs off the sea. (Now, Rossi's theater recalls them.) Out of another common vernacular, that of the strip, Venturi's firehouse at Columbus, Indiana, calls to us from the side of the road (106). The environment comes alive with the endlessly complicated actions of people in situations or with their simple presence. Magic Realist painting is similar (107). The everyday environment is fraught with being, sometimes with irony, sometimes with love. Painting, sculpture, and architecture here all seem to share a renewed sense of common life. Nothing can be boring because all is living. One is tempted to feel that if there is any real hope for the future it lies in our perception of that.

Venturi, to go further, seems always to have

101

107

102

GUILD HOUSE

103

101   Louis I. Kahn, Indian Institute of Management, Ahmedabad, 1964–1966.

102   Robert Venturi, main entrance, Guild House, Philadelphia, 1960–1963.

103   Duane Hanson, Woman Eating, with artist, ca. 1970.

104   Robert Venturi, Trubek and Wislocki houses, Nantucket, Massachusetts, 1972.

105   Robert Venturi, front view, Wislocki house, Nantucket, Massachusetts.

106   Robert Venturi, Fire Station No. 4, Columbus, Indiana, 1965–1967.

107   John Baeder, The Pullman, 1974.

108   Robert Venturi, design for Franklin D. Roosevelt Memorial, 1960.

109   Michael Heizer, "Double Negative" at Virgin River Mesa, Nevada, 1969.

106

104

105

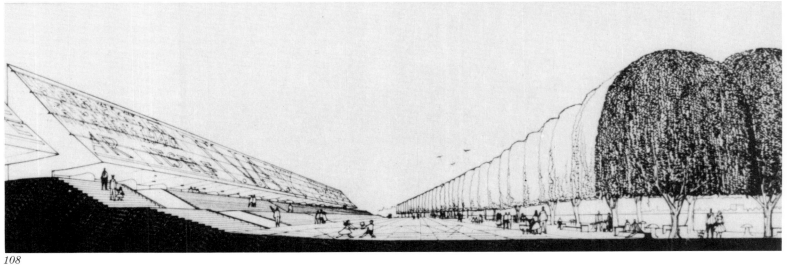

108

109

110

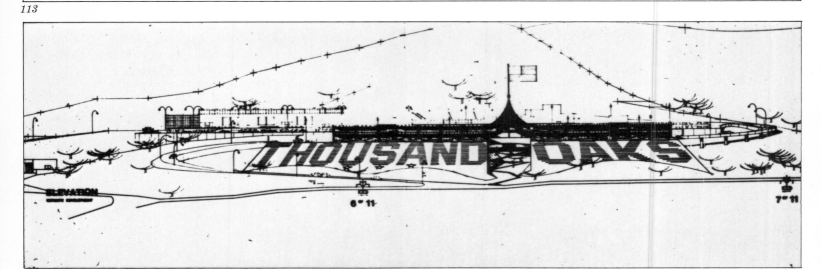
113

111

110  Karl Ehn, Heiligenstadt
Housing, Karl Marx Hof
Vienna, 1927.

111  Robert Venturi, project for
urban center, Thousand Oaks,
California, 1969.

112  Robert Venturi, center section, project for urban center,
Thousand Oaks, California.

113  Robert Venturi, design for
National Football Hall of
Fame, 1967.

114  Robert Venturi, perspective drawing of interior, design
for National Football Hall of
Fame.

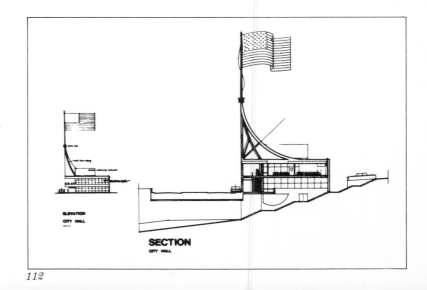
112

understood the dual realities of environment and
act. His Roosevelt Memorial entry is environmental
sculpture, a great earthwork (108). In this it not
only invokes the gardens and the fortifications of
the classic tradition in which Venturi was trained
but also prefigures the earth sculptures, like those
of Heizer, of the decade which was to follow (109).
Venturi can also challenge the environment with
forms that seem to menace it, like his unexploded
shell for Fairmount Parkway, not explicitly ironic
like Oldenburg's great toilet floats for London but
intrusive like them, inserting another order of being
into the urban scene. By contrast, environment and
act are unified in Venturi's project for the town
center of Thousand Oaks, California, sweeping along
the freeway and lifting up its flag, like those on the
Karl Marx Hof in Vienna, to be seen not by nearby
pedestrians but by drivers closing in at suicidal
rates of speed (110, 111, 112). So the graphics of the
older project, an essential component of its
emotional effect, are enlarged to highway scale and
change their sense as we draw up to them and read
only part of their sign. This is indeed sculpture,
architecture, and painting all together.

In complementary action to the two kinds of
physical being—that of creatures and that of
places—comes painting's world of illusion where all
can be brought together through optical means.
Venturi showed how that resource could function in
his competition for the National Football Hall of
Fame. All its forms are in accord with existing
reality, and all are transformed. The cars come up
and park in great waves. Above them a tremendous
electronic signboard, like the screen of a drive-in
theater, presents memorable plays, relives historic
situations; the backs run and are tackled like giant
constellations across the face of the night (113).
Piano & Rogers originally intended such a screen on
the plaza facade of the Centre Pompidou and cited
this project as their prototype. Inside, the fixed
exhibits were to have been supplemented by movie
projection through which the boundaries of the
space are dissolved (114). Soon lasers could have
conjured up three-dimensional holographs of solid
figures in the middle of the air. In this way painting
joins architecture and sculpture at the height of its
contemporary freedom to "make us see what isn't
there," and the fact of collaboration—not the old
ideal of it but the present fact of it—is achieved. As
the Romans opened out the whole wall through
perspective long ago and as nineteenth-century
scenic wallpapers made the most spectacular
topographies of the globe readily available through
mass production, so now illusions invade our space
and pull us into theirs. The dweller in the ten-foot
room of a conceivable future might walk one day in
the gardens of Vaux-le-Vicomte and descend the
next to the Colorado in the depths of its canyon or
travel for many days in arduous stages across the
Sahara or struggle with the wheel of a clipper ship
through a long, bad passage round the Horn. There
will always be those of us who are suspicious of such
ease of electronic creation, but the history of art

114

shows us that the human mind can deal with whatever the techniques of its art can fabricate for it. From the moment the bosses of the cave ceiling at Altamira were transformed through painting into bison, the doors to all other worlds have been open. Only power is essential, whether from the shoulder or the turbine. If the latter should fail, art might well fall back again to the pine board we whittle in our hands. And not much would be lost. A universe could be shaped and populated with that as well, though in another way.

To return to more immediate questions: a number of contemporary architects other than Venturi have shown themselves to be aware of the issues of act and environment and of their implications for architectural form. Moore, for example, believes in the primacy of the physical experience of architecture, which he calls the "haptic," and he designs houses which are buoyant frames for human action, especially in the vertical dimension. He has confidence in the ability of human beings to decide things for themselves and is unfailingly amused by the results. He goes on television to induce the citizens of wherever he may be to make specific suggestions about whatever urban project he is involved with according to their own concept of what they want to do in a place, and his designs for public spaces take special cognizance of such interrelationships, seen through the model of play. They convey a great deal by making it all seem a playful assemblage, like the Piazza d'Italia in New Orleans (115). So columns, entablatures, and inscriptions can be piled up in ways widely acceptable because it all appears to be harmless fun. Water gushes forth, cascades, and leaps in sparkling sheets, uniting everything. Like the Baroque which Moore knows so well, the conflict between will to order and will to anarchy is glossed over. The issue doesn't seem important because everything really is decoration once again.

In Graves the issue is joined with deep seriousness. His house projects are intensely environmental. Indeed, they stretch out across the landscape and hollow out grottoes and bosquets in a perhaps mythical forest. They are also intensely sculptural in that their massively active elements may often seem to be attacking the general architectural order (116). This is a supremely Mannerist condition, and it is a fundamental reason why colossal Mannerist rustication, rather than the flowing profiles of the Baroque, seems to possess a special appeal for many architects now. Of all those architects Graves is the boldest and strongest. Like Giulio Romano, he may make his keystones seem to fall, his doorways split, his facades crumble. Decoration revolts; it attacks the building. The architectural environment is under assault by Titanic sculptural forces. Finally, though, the whole is still largely pictorial, because so much is in fact taking place upon a single plane, illusionistically endowed with depth. Sculpture's

116

115  Charles Moore, Piazza
d'Italia, New Orleans, Loui-
siana, 1978–1979.

116  Michael Graves, elevation
of central bridge, Fargo-Moor-
head Cultural Center, Fargo,
North Dakota, and Moorhead,
Minnesota, 1977–1978.

117  Michael Graves, elevation,
Public Services Building, Portland, Oregon, 1980.

118

119

120

primitive force is marvelously evoked, as in a Mannerist grotto, but the mood, as there, is a Romantic one, richly melancholy. Now, Graves' project for the Portland Public Office Building in Portland, Oregon, so cruelly savaged by the criticism of local architects, moves out into a grander realm of Mannerist intransigence, involving powerful architectural decoration with figural sculpture at enormous scale (117). There are surely many problems of suitability and relationship as yet unresolved in this stupendous assemblage, but for all that it is a great, indeed an epoch-making work, strange and courageous, and it very much deserves to be built as Graves designed it.

Stern, too, as in his project for Best Products, seems aware of the issue. He clearly tries to bring it back as close as he yet dares to its classic context and vocabulary. In this we come again to that question which has been one of the minor themes of the argument. How far back can we go? One of the criteria, perhaps, might be fitness, the old classical "propriety." And in this category, like almost all the other entries in the Best's exhibition, Stern's project may be said to fail. Because of the very richness of its admirable iconography it is literally top-heavy, trying to say too much for the program; it has too much sign for the building. This is what Venturi apparently understood in the same program; sometimes wallpaper, properly scaled, is just right and enough, and more classic in "decorum" than pediments, stoas, or Palladian windows.

It may indeed be taken as true that things never happen as we expect them to or give us quite the ideal that we hoped for. This is because we can only imagine the reality with which we are familiar and can rarely recognize the new reality when it arrives. Our conceptual screens, through which our minds filter all phenomena, have to change first. That is, I think, one reason at least why it is worthwhile to write about art: to struggle with that process. It is the fundamental human problem of growth, which involves how to break our own preexisting models of reality in order to be able to ask the new questions out of which knowledge can grow. We have, for example, been able to think our way back to an appreciation of Beaux-Arts architecture and its collaborative achievement, and beyond that to the fundamental question of ornament as a whole. Is that the end of our search? How lovely it might be if Greenberg's dream of the return to the classic tradition, straight, noble, unparodied, could be realized (118, 119). Will it ever be? What sculpture will adorn or challenge it? What painting? Though no less real an image of human action than those shaped by the Greeks, could a tourist by Duane Hanson really stand in a pediment, peering out across the parkway? Could Baeder paint it? Perhaps. But if not, we should ask ourselves why not. And the answer seems to be that there might well be some sort of consciousness lacking, something real about things as we feel them to be in Hanson, Baeder, Heizer, and Venturi which is not there. Some irony perhaps but most of all some comment. So Venturi comments about the historical styles when he employs them: turns them into cutouts, or changes their scale, or blows out the color. He parodies them, as of course do Moore, Graves, and Stern, which to Greenberg is a deplorable thing. But for all the distortions and through them, Venturi shows us what the issues are: how the act is embodied in a building, though it remains environment (120). Once again, correctness is not enough, if it ever was. But propriety and decorum still play the critical parts, so that a screen of Greek columns by Venturi takes on the touchingly wistful presence of the American Greek Revival (120—big act, little building) and is then flattened out and stretched in accordance with the volumetric space and thin wall structure of the Shingle Style vernacular itself (121). The comment is double and in the end, to revive a ghostly term, functionally right. Act and environment are in the tension of life.

There can be no doubt that the historicism of the Modern Movement, which said that we could not do this or that because our times would not let us, must be rejected. Existentialism taught us once and for all that we are the times. We make them; we are responsible for them. We cannot hide from that necessity for action and choice in the arms of the zeitgeist. But we do in fact feel things in certain ways. Artists of course will always see things afresh and will inevitably surprise us and so change our feelings. The classical sculptor who will place Apollo on a classical pediment may be honing his chisel at this moment. Another Poussin may be assiduously reading Ovid, Livy, and the Bible and sharpening his pencil. Still, one doesn't really think so. The academic synthesis no longer responds to the depth, breadth, and critical awareness of our consciousness. Nor, as the Post-Modernists so correctly insist, should we expect to have only one style of art or one synthesis of styles. Instead we will probably have as many styles of art as we have of life, most of them contradictory of each other. The word "style" will be devalued, as it probably ought to be. We have already liberated ourselves from that concept through our wreck of the International Style. The feeling is of a new freedom but not of a new salvation. There will be no new, soul-saving synthesis. We must get used to the fact that we have lost our souls and, as Picasso so instinctively seems to say, are now forced to find our way back to fellowship with our mutilated brothers, the animals. No, the soul as an item of distinction is finished, but there will be the physical arts, taking shape out of whatever programs and materials they can find. We should face the fact that they are now our cult. We will always have to shape our environment in one way or another with them, preferably, in future, with solar and other nondestructive sources of power. We will be required to populate that environment and to act in certain ways. We will surely seek to explore new modes of being through the pictorial imagination which is the very stuff of our dreams. The questions so laid bare will always be relevant to us and will provoke all our arts. They may be arts of agony, derision, or sorrow. We ask ourselves if they will be able to collaborate with each other or will tear us with their autonomous frenzies. That will depend on us, because we are not dominated, as some of our mentors may have seemed to think in the past, by any overwhelming inevitability in human history or in the forms of art. We are what we make ourselves. The art of the future will be what we have become.

It is reasonable to take a pessimistic view of the outcome. A critic can hardly fail to do so. But experience shows that the artist is incurably optimistic. He composes if necessary out of disaster and decay. He has little to do with the good or the desirable, with ethical structures or ideologies. He knows with a fierce physical certainty that, as Oscar Wilde put it, "The aesthetic reaction has nothing to do with the intellect, or the emotions." It bursts free. In its service the artist twists everything to his own ends, which are ruthless ones. He *will* make forms, no matter what, and out of our worst defeats fashion other dreams, worlds, and populations to come.

121

118   Allan Greenberg, Superior Court Building, Manchester, Connecticut, 1980.

119   Allan Greenberg, project for a country house in Connecticut, 1979–1980.

120   Robert Venturi, Eclectic House, 1977.

121   Robert Venturi, west elevation, Flint House, Centerville, Maryland, 1978.

# Part 2

# The Present

"The complete building is the final aim of the visual arts. Their noblest function was once the decoration of the buildings. Today they exist in isolation, from which they can be rescued only through the conscious co-operative effort of all craftsmen. Architects, painters and sculptors must recognize anew the composite character of a building as an entity. Only then will their work be imbued with the architectonic spirit which it has lost as 'salon art.' "

So read the manifesto of the Bauhaus, the earnest, if innocent, testament of 1919 against Victorian and Edwardian architecture which was to act as a clarion call to the developing Modern Movement. No matter that the integration of art and architecture had actually been one of the very principles upon which the Beaux-Arts architecture, rejected by the Bauhaus, had depended; the violent dislike of decoration, of ornament, of all things historicist that motivated the Bauhaus's founders led them to denounce virtually all the output of the period from which they emerged. Their dispute was not with art, but with academic art, with representational art, and the call for change that they issued was to become, implicitly if not explicitly, the rationale behind virtually all the collaborations between artists and architects in the years to follow.

The manifesto was, in brief, an assertion of the superiority of architecture. To create a "complete building" was seen as the ultimate purpose not only of architecture, but of all the visual arts. The other arts were never so noble as when they were created to serve architecture, the manifesto says, and it speaks in almost melodramatic terms of the "rescue" of the visual arts from their sad fate of solitary existence away from architecture. The values they need are the "architectonic" ones; other values, it would seem, have no place.

The history of the Bauhaus itself is not, of course, our concern here, and it should only be noted that the school's various masters produced a substantial amount of important art that was neither particularly architectonic nor the result of any unusual degree of collaboration. Nonetheless, the spirit behind the manifesto certainly seemed to summarize, if not also to have had a part in creating, the attitude of architects toward the work of artists in the decades of the Bauhaus's greatest influence. It set the tone for those years—not, of course, the decades of the Bauhaus's actual existence, but those which followed, the 1940s, 1950s, and 1960s. Then, not in its lively, prickly adolescence, but in a priggish and self-assured middle age, did Modernism triumph.

These decades, for all the talk of true collaboration, were fundamentally times of art placed *in* buildings, not art made of and from and about particular works of architecture or, more important, the reverse—architecture made *for* particular works of art. There was little of that, and there was little enough of any sense that art was being created to comment in some way about the qualities and meaning of a specific place. Most of the "collaborations," even the most successful ones, were in fact juxtapositions more than anything else—they were works of art placed within works of architecture, with the chief role of sculpture being to fill the space and the chief role of painting being to distract our eye and provide visual relief.

It is no accident, then, that the image of architectural sculpture that comes most quickly to the layperson's mind, if not also to the artist's, is that of a Henry Moore figure placed in front of a crisp, solid geometric building, such as I.M. Pei's library at Columbus, Indiana, of 1969, his East Building of the National Gallery of Art in Washington, D.C., of 1978, or his Dallas City Hall of 1978. In each case the work of art exists as a kind of antidote to the architecture—as a lightening device, as a softener. The plastic forms of the Moore sculpture provide a formal counterpoint to the hard edges of the building, suggesting that the architect's desire was not solely to create harsh forms. The Moore functions as a response to the question so often posed about the hard and heavy geometric forms of post-war Modernism—it says that the architect does respect humanist values and that he does seek to have them present in his work.

Nevertheless, in a purely architectural sense, these buildings were complete works before the Moore sculptures were put into place, and in this way they are no different from the mediocre apartment tower erected on Park Avenue in New

# Toward Different Ends

*By Paul Goldberger*

York in 1976 which has a small Henry Moore placed beside its front door, not suggesting communication between artist and architect so much as it is demonstrating that the building, for all the banality of its physical appearance, is in fact inhabited by cultivated people. Even more obviously such a case is the Henry Moore that was placed in front of the Hirshhorn Museum in Washington, D.C., of 1974 by Skidmore, Owings & Merrill (SOM). The building is a round concrete cylinder that looks like an oil tank more than a civic monument, and here the Moore functions like a sign, reminding us that this *is*, in fact, a museum. It is perhaps a tribute to Henry Moore that his work is able to do so as clearly as a flashing neon sign reading "Art Inside."

The Henry Moore at the Hirshhorn does provide, like those in front of the Pei buildings, a pleasing counterpoint to the forms and geometries of the building itself, and it is a handsome work. But its role as a sign is what is most striking—and what tells us, unfortunately, the most about the relationship of architecture to sculpture and art in the decades since 1945. For these have been years in which the value of public art has not been seriously questioned (despite the vociferous battles over public financing of certain projects as well as battles over aesthetics) and in which, indeed, art has come to be an expected part of most major public structures. But there has been relatively little in the way of true collaboration, and instead, much of what has occurred has followed the underlying values of the Bauhaus manifesto. We have seen architecture take the lead, with art and sculpture subservient—added to the complete or near-complete work of architecture as a counterpoint to its forms or merely as a sign telling us that culture lies within. What we have seen is juxtaposition more than collaboration.

But rare indeed have been the works of architecture that one feels have been made complete, rendered whole, by works of painting or sculpture that have been made for them. Even some of the finest works of art of this period within some of the finest works of architecture have been unable to do this; they seem unable to convince us that they could exist just as well someplace else, that their presence within a particular work of architecture is both vital to their own artistic integrity and vital to the meaning of that work of architecture. In this sense they violate the letter of the Bauhaus manifesto in its call for true collaboration, but follow instead the unstated implication of those lines, which rendered architecture primary.

These trends were evident at the beginning of the post-war period. Rockefeller Center, one of the last great works of pre-war American architecture, is lavishly filled with art which seems, whatever its own merits, to be intrinsic to the architecture; if works such as the bas-relief atop the entrance to the RCA Building can be criticized at all, it is that they are not a little melodramatic and decorative. But that bas-relief enhances and deepens the architecture of the building; it does not stand apart from the themes of the RCA tower, and it is difficult to imagine the experience of visiting the building as being quite the same without the bas-relief. One might say the same for the murals within the lobby, weak as they are by comparison to the original set by Diego Rivera which was removed for political reasons; although the murals do not change the dimensions of the space, they alter its texture and its tone and thus play a significant role in shaping its mood.

One might contrast this with the Terrace Plaza (now Terrace Hilton) Hotel in Cincinnati by Skidmore, Owings & Merrill, completed in 1948. An innovative building—it includes an eight-story retail base below the hotel—the building had murals by Joan Miró (1) and Saul Steinberg (2) in the restaurants and a mobile by Alexander Calder in the lobby. The works are all sprightly and fresh, right for the tensile, bright mood of this new hotel, but one can already feel a movement away from the sense of integration present at Rockefeller Center. The murals enhance and support a mood, but the tone is clearly set by the architecture. And the Calder mobile, breath of fresh air as it must have been for the hotel business in 1948, seemed to prefigure the uses to which Moore's sculpture would be put—plastic forms to serve as counterpoint to hard edges.

1   *Joan Miró, dining room mural, Terrace Plaza Hotel, Cincinnati, Ohio, 1948.*

2   *Saul Steinberg, dining room mural, Terrace Plaza Hotel, Cincinnati, Ohio, 1948.*

The Terrace Plaza was influential, and properly so, for however much the mix of architecture and art may have been less than truly collaborative, the decision by a major real-estate developer to commission such works of art in a commercial project of this type could only make such decisions easier for other projects in the future. And Skidmore, Owings & Merrill, then at the brink of a remarkable several decades as one of the nation's preeminent commercial architectural practices, was to be a force for greater and more elaborate collaborations with artists in the years to follow.

Indeed, much of the history of the collaboration between architects and artists, in terms of large-scale works at least, is a history of SOM's efforts. In 1954, for example, the firm's epoch-making glass bank for the Manufacturers Trust Company on Fifth Avenue in New York (now Manufacturers Hanover Trust Company) opened, containing a 70-foot long metal sculpture by Harry Bertoia. The work is an intricate screen composed of a vast number of tiny metal panels of gold and bronze tone; it was commissioned by Gordon Bunshaft, the Skidmore partner who designed the bank, and he and Bertoia worked closely together. The work shimmers in a way that suggests the themes of the architecture of the little glass box of which it is a part, so the aesthetics are certainly compatible between building and artwork; the Bertoia's impact on the overall feeling of the bank is not, however, particularly strong. Bunshaft's glass box is so striking that it overwhelms the piece, which seems, in the end, more a weak echo of the architecture than a true partner to it. Far more powerful, ironically, is the great round Mosler safe that was placed right beside the glass wall to stun passersby—it is the real work of sculpture here and the only object that seems able to conduct a true aesthetic dialogue with the building.

So Bertoia, in the end, was providing decoration more than anything else. Oddly, Fernand Léger, in his murals in the United Nations General Assembly Building, managed to do more; the bulging forms of Léger's two-dimensional works really do seem to have mass, and they enhance and deepen the quality of the space of which they are a part. Little else at the United Nations is so successful—the

Barbara Hepworth sculpture in front of the glass Secretariat tower functions as do the Henry Moores, as a plastic object which its donors hoped, obviously, would play off against the lines of the building itself. It does so, but the architecture and the sculpture are too far apart aesthetically to do much except play a kind of catch with one another; the eye bounces back and forth, and there is no real connection, no sense of engaging dialogue.

More ambitious, to move to the late 1950s and early 1960s, were the art and architecture collaborations in the design of Lincoln Center, the performing arts complex in New York City. The overall grouping of buildings suggests that of the Capitoline hill in Rome, but in New York two things are missing—the buildings are set at precise right angles to each other, losing the movement and energy established by their slightly acute angles at Rome, and the central space is occupied not by a sculptural figure but by a fountain, an object that, for all the visual and aural pleasure it offers, cannot control the space with any real force. Oddly here as at the Manufacturers Bank, an accident takes over—the two huge murals by Marc Chagall, which fill the blank front ends of the Metropolitan Opera House's two side service wings, bring the real movement and color to the central square. They are weak works in themselves, and they surely did not emerge out of a real collaboration—they were commissioned late in the game, after a redesign of the opera house led to the appearance of these walls—but they do bring considerable life to this outdoor plaza.

The other outdoor sculpture at Lincoln Center consists of two major works quite common for the period—a black Calder stabile and a Henry Moore reclining figure. In each case the juxtaposition of art and architecture is successful, if only because here the counterpoint the sculpture provides is direct enough to communicate strongly and has certain subtle overtones. The strong horizontal lines of the Vivian Beaumont Theater by Eero Saarinen and the long reaches of the reflecting pool frame and enclose the Moore, for example, making it stronger. In the case of the Calder, the vertical ribs, or fins, on the side of the opera house, rather

4

5

pointless decoration on their own, create a striping that enhances the Calder by giving it a stronger, crisper background against which to respond.

The interior works of art—the Chagalls—despite their presence indoors, really affect the outdoors and are less successful. Elie Nadelman's two immense *Seated Ladies* in the great foyer of the New York State Theater by Philip Johnson are grotesquely overscaled; their size is right for the space but not for themselves, and so they must rank as yet another example of sculpture subjugated to the demands of architecture. At Avery Fisher (formerly Philharmonic) Hall by Max Abramovitz, Richard Lippold's set of brass slabs suspended in space in the multistoried lobby is diverting and lively and surely fills up the huge hall—but this is a case in which there seems to be no real power either to the architecture or to the art. Both are rather decorative, and if the sculpture can be said to have any major virtue, it is that it distracts the eye from the architecture of the space.

Lippold, whose commitment to architectural sculpture has been serious and genuine, was more successful in a slightly earlier project, the sculpture for the Grill Room of the Four Seasons Restaurant in the Seagram Building in New York. Here hundreds of hanging rods over the bar make not only for a beautiful object, but for one that seems, almost intuitively, to be right for its place—they suggest, without ever being coyingly literal, the forms of glasses and mixing sticks. More significant is how the sculpture, which has a smaller echo of itself hung diagonally across the room, brings a shimmering movement to the room, enhancing the play of light and shadow and counterposing in just the right way the oak paneling which lines the walls. At the Four Seasons Lippold's aesthetic was precisely in tune with that of Philip Johnson, the architect, and he was able to complement and enrich it through his work.

Eero Saarinen's late work, Ezra Stiles and Morse colleges at Yale University, was in design in the late 1950s and finished in 1961. Here Saarinen commissioned Constantino Nivola to create a series of freestanding sculptures as well as bas-reliefs to be made of concrete and integrated into the

*3*

*3  Josef Albers, mosaic mural
developed from artist's abstract
design called* Reclining Figure,
*Celanese Building, Rockefeller
Center, New York, 1973.*

*4  Josef Albers, Portals, Time
& Life Building, Rockefeller
Center, New York, 1961.*

*5  Fritz Glarner, Relational
Painting #88, Time & Life
Building, Rockefeller Center,
New York, 1960.*

6

6  *Isamu Noguchi,* Chase Manhattan Bank Plaza Garden, *New York, 1961–1964.*

7  *Isamu Noguchi,* Beinecke Rare Book and Manuscript Library Garden, *Yale University, New Haven, Connecticut, 1960–1964.*

7

residential complex in New Haven. The bas-reliefs are significant in that they suggest a return to the literal, physical integration of sculpture and architecture that had existed in the Beaux-Arts influenced work of the late nineteenth and early twentieth centuries and reappeared in such unusual works as the late buildings of Bertram Goodhue in the 1920s, for example. But here the little abstract bas-reliefs, playful in their curves and yet somehow all too serious at the same time, seemed not so much to emerge naturally out of the architecture as to have been tacked on. One gets the impression that their removal might lead to a hole in the wall, but not to a diminished work of architecture. This is in considerable contrast with an earlier collaboration in which Saarinen was involved, the chapel for the Massachusetts Institute of Technology at Cambridge completed in 1955. Here a Theodore Roszak bell tower, an abstraction of a traditional church spire, turns Saarinen's simple building from a plain drum into a work of religious architecture. Similarly, Harry Bertoia's altar screen, not altogether different from his unsatisfactory work at the Manufacturers Bank, here seems to glow with a sense of real purpose—it is related especially well to the skylights that bring natural light into the chapel, which it filters and reflects. In both cases Saarinen worked closely with the sculptors, and the results suggest that neither architect nor sculptors could have produced such successful works alone.

One cannot say the same for another Nivola work, quite similar to his effort with Saarinen at Yale. This was a set of pieces set into a blank brick wall at Public School 33 in Brooklyn, designed by Frederick G. Frost; Nivola's bas-reliefs decorate, but they do not change, and it is difficult to see what effect they have on the architecture that a group of bricks projecting from the wall plane where the tiny sculptures now are mounted would not have.

This Nivola was one of many pieces to emerge in the 1950s out of an ambitious program that involved major artists in the design of New York City public schools. The results, unfortunately, were rarely better than at P.S. 33 and in no case did they suggest a true collaboration. The artist was brought in after the building was designed and assigned a space which he or she would decorate, though that word would surely have been anathema to the well-intentioned participants in this program. Where the results were successful, it was largely because a lively work of art could bring a certain spirit to a pedestrian building, as Mary Callery's rhythmic steel sculpture, representing figures from the fables of La Fontaine, does at P.S. 34 in Manhattan designed by Harrison & Abramovitz, or Gwen Lux's tensile steel sculpture, *Vapor Trails*, does for Aviation High School in Queens, designed by Chapman, Evans & Delahunty. But the school system could crush even the most inventive of artists, it seemed—a Hans Hofmann mosaic wall at the New York School of Printing, by Kelly & Gruzen, seems flat and dull.

The mosaic wall and the mural were to remain popular devices for so-called collaborations through the 1950s and 1960s. But too often at this time the artists merely echoed the abstractions of the architecture, as Josef Albers—incidentally a former Bauhaus master—did at the Celanese Building in Rockefeller's westward extension (3–4), not completed until 1972, or Fritz Glarner did in his colorful Time-Life Building lobby mural of 1958 (5). Both are welcome infusions of color in rather cold architecture, but little else; there is not even that formal contrast that more plastic works such as the Henry Moore sculptures bring to hard-edged architecture. Albers did somewhat better in the lobby of the Corning Glass Building on Fifth Avenue in New York of 1958, but here again the architecture—in each case by Harrison & Abramovitz—is not really affected by the art.

It was Skidmore, Owings & Merrill in the 1960s that was to produce the most effective collaborations, at least at large scale. Isamu Noguchi's stark sculptures for the below-grade "gardens"—that is to say, sunken plazas—at the Chase Manhattan Bank headquarters in New York of 1961 (6) and at the Beinecke Library at Yale of 1963 (7) were both effective works, whatever the merits of the awkward surroundings the architect, Gordon Bunshaft, had given them. In each case Noguchi managed to create a work that enriched and deepened the quality of the space in which it was set, a work that could not in itself have had the meaning it gained from this context.

Of course, the contexts themselves were only partly architectural. In each case there was a large building that rose from a stark concrete plaza; Noguchi's sunken gardens were cut into the plazas a fair distance from the above-ground structures, to which they bear no relation at all. So the collaboration, effective as it is, is not really with the total building—it is with half a building, some distance away.

Noguchi and Gordon Bunshaft did better a few years later at 140 Broadway, a block away from Chase in lower Manhattan, completed in 1967 (8). This may rank as the finest commercial collaboration of the decade: Noguchi's orange cube, balanced on a corner and cut through by a cylindrical hole, completes and enhances Bunshaft's sleek dark glass tower. The tower is one of Bunshaft's few truly graceful buildings; it has a skin that is more refined, yet also less articulated, than that of Chase Manhattan. The orange cube is itself somewhat sleek, so there is enough similarity to permit a sense of real communication between the work of sculpture and its background, making it clear that this is in no way a case of the sculpture as antidote to the aesthetic of the building. Yet the sculpture does, in fact, offer contrasts to the building: where the tower is dull, it is bright; where the tower appears solid, it appears unbalanced. The tower, elegant as it is, would have far less meaning without the cube, and the cube would be a much less potent work without this setting. One need only look at sculptor Tony Rosenthal's *Cube*, a similar but more complex work balanced on a corner at Cooper Square in New York; despite the more elaborate nature of Rosenthal's cube, it in fact appears to be a simpler work because it lacks the presence of a definable, relatively similar context which it can engage in dialogue.

Moreover, Bunshaft and Noguchi worked in true collaboration here; they tried several versions of the work, and it was Bunshaft who selected the single large cube on end after rejecting arrangements of smaller cubes. The discovery of the right form came after an initial start with an arrangement of rocks, not unlike the Chase Manhattan work, which would have yielded a far less subtle dialogue with the Bunshaft building. For what is so special here is that the cube and the building represent a similar, but not identical, aesthetic; they are close enough in intention to seem almost the same, and it is in their subtle differences that their true aesthetic dialogue emerges.

The Bunshaft-Noguchi collaboration has no precise equivalent in American architecture in recent decades—in no other case can the work of a respected architect be said to have been so completed, so made whole, by the work of an equally respected artist. Most of the Bunshaft-Noguchi efforts, by the nature of Bunshaft's standing as a partner in the New York office of Skidmore, Owings & Merrill, took place in New York City or elsewhere on the East Coast. Oddly, while New York's record in the 1960s as a city hospitable to quality architecture was not the best, it probably did achieve the most noteworthy collaborations. In other cities there are only sporadic successes. There is little in the way of major public sculpture in Houston, for example, despite the immense outpouring of new construction there; efforts have been made at improving that city's climate for collaboration, but so far they have borne little fruit. The best work of public sculpture at this point is Claes Oldenburg's *Mouse* in front of the Houston Public Library, designed by Eugene Aubrey of S.I. Morris Associates and completed in 1977. The Aubrey building is a hard-edged set of geometric forms, not altogether different in its aesthetic from I.M. Pei's East Building of the National Gallery of Art; surprisingly, the red Oldenburg plays a role not unlike that of the Henry Moore in front of the Pei building, acting as a counterpoint to the sharp forms of the architecture. But there is a sense of whimsy to the Oldenburg altogether lacking in the Moore works, and it gives the collaboration life.

Los Angeles, San Francisco, and Minneapolis, to name three other cities in which architecture of note was produced during this period, are similarly devoid of major efforts at collaboration.

8

8  Isamu Noguchi, Red Cube,
*Marine Midland Building, New
York, 1968.*

Minneapolis is blessed with good works within its buildings, such as the Andy Warhol prints commissioned for the Marquette Inn, the hotel designed by Philip Johnson and John Burgee as part of their IDS Center and completed in 1972. But while Warhol's rising sun image is ideal for the brightly colored Johnson and Burgee rooms, this can hardly be called a significant collaborative effort.

Remaining in the Midwest, one might consider Eero Saarinen's great arch in St. Louis, completed in 1963, to be a kind of monumental sculpture—it surely affects the environment in sculptural more than architectural terms, dominating the city with a pure abstraction in a way that no real building could do. It is startlingly beautiful, but what it is unable to do is relate comfortably to the rest of the city—it is so large that it makes the real buildings below it seem like toys, and it seems like a form that would be more comfortable on the plains in a pure and neutral landscape.

Washington, D.C., has not done much better in terms of recent collaborations. The city's powerful Beaux-Arts orientation has tended to be an inhibiting factor so far as a great deal of modern design has been concerned; it was not until the East Building of the National Gallery that Washington had a truly first-rate modern building at civic scale. The city's coolness toward the winning scheme in the Franklin D. Roosevelt memorial competition, an essentially sculptural composition by Pederson & Tilney, was not altogether surprising, then—the project, a set of standing plaques with quotations from Roosevelt carved onto their faces, was far too abstract to be welcomed easily by a city whose idea of a memorial remained a Henry Bacon Greek temple with a Daniel Chester French figure inside. But while the rejection of the scheme by the Roosevelt family was widely criticized as an act of hostility toward modern architecture, it is only fair to observe that, whatever the virtues of the Pederson scheme, its strong abstractions were not easily related to the existing architectural context of the capital city. This was clearly not a case of collaboration, but rather, once again, one of juxtaposition.

Chicago is one city in which major public sculpture has had significant impact—although here again, there is a real question as to the extent of the actual collaboration involved. In three cases large works have been placed in association with major downtown skyscrapers—a Calder stabile in the plaza of Mies van der Rohe's Federal Center of 1969; a Picasso in the plaza in front of the Chicago Civic Center (9), by C. F. Murphy Associates and Skidmore, Owings & Merrill of 1967; and a mosaic by Marc Chagall on a long freestanding wall in front of the First National Bank of Chicago by C. F. Murphy and Perkins & Will of 1969. The Calder is the most successful: its bright orange color dances against Mies's somber facades, and its leaping forms manage to control and define the large plaza space, sending it into just the right degree of movement.

The Picasso, like the Nadelmans at the New York State Theater, seems too large for itself; it is a more coherent work at smaller scale, and this problem prevents it from being as articulate as it might be before the huge Cor-ten steel tower—though the work is well scaled to the tower itself and has also done more, perhaps, than any major piece of public sculpture in any American downtown to stimulate a public dialogue on the value of such collaborative efforts. In any event the Picasso's images are far more powerful than those of the Chagall mosaic, which is pretty but essentially without real impact. Its long wall succeeds better than the mosaic itself at playing off against the harsh concrete curves of the immense bank tower.

These last two works give the impression of being able to be anywhere. They are not alone in having this quality—that became an especially serious problem in these years as the drive to place works by major artists in positions of prominence led to a great number of works being commissioned without any real connection to the architecture which was to be their surrounding. Calder's mechanical sculpture in the lobby of the Sears Tower by Skidmore, Owings & Merrill in Chicago of 1974, called *Universe*, seems almost like a temporary display, brought in to add some color

9

9   *Picasso, Chicago Picasso,*
*Chicago Civic Center, 1967.*

10  *Charles Perry, Eclipse,*
*Hyatt Regency Hotel, San*
*Francisco, 1973.*

and movement to the sterile marble tomb that is the lobby of the world's tallest office building. Indeed, this was a more common fate for Calder's architectural sculptures in those years than the successful relationship achieved at the Chicago Federal Center; Calders came to be considered automatic devices capable of enlivening dull places and serving, like the works of Henry Moore, as signposts, as proofs that the values of culture had not been forgotten.

But even sculptors without Calder's or Moore's degree of popular acceptance could fall victim to the problem of seeing their work inserted into surroundings to which it bore no relation. Claes Oldenburg's *Batcolumn* in Chicago, for example, a sculpture in the form of a baseball bat, was placed in front of a banal federal building in 1978; it surely enlivens the building, but both the sculpture and the architecture exist in their own worlds, free of any real need for each other. One might say the same for Oldenburg's *Clothespin*, near City Hall in Philadelphia, though here the sculpture itself is more powerful by far than the one in Chicago, and its juxtaposition next to existing works of architecture is all the more startling. The *Clothespin* is strong enough, indeed, to pull together the diverse elements of its context and to alter one's perceptions of all the surrounding buildings, despite the fact that the art and the architecture seem to have independent existences. Just as independent, yet more powerful still as a result of the small scale of its context, is Oldenburg's *Lipstick* in the courtyard of Morse College at Yale—where not the least of the things it does is render Nivola's work still weaker.

If scale assists Oldenburg's *Lipstick*, it makes the task of communicating impossible for some other works. As the size and scale of contemporary architecture have grown, sculptors and architects have been faced with a difficult choice—to expand the size of their works to be compatible with the architecture of which they are in part, at which point they risk permitting their works to overwhelm the observer as much as does the architecture, or to keep their works small, risking their virtual obliteration by immense buildings. The

sculptors who have worked with John Portman in the creation of his early Hyatt Regency Hotels of the mid-1960s chose the first route; the sphere entitled *Eclipse* by Charles Perry in the atrium of the San Francisco Hyatt at the Embarcadero Center (10) is certainly in scale with the vast space, but it is awesome in size to the observer—not to mention utterly banal. It is a work that might, however, have had more meaning at smaller scale in a different context where it could have had some purpose other than the mere filling of space. The opposite problem befell Alexander Calder when a stabile was placed behind the towers of the World Trade Center in Manhattan—the buildings are so big that the sculpture looks like a toy, even from close up.

The World Trade Center's huge plaza and twin 110-story towers cannot really be a hospitable context for any sculpture—no building at that scale can accommodate works of sculpture except those that are so vast as to be awesome and intimidating in themselves. The globe by Fritz Koenig in the middle of the center's plaza suffers in both ways— it is at once too big to be read easily as a work of sculpture and too small to anchor the vast towers that rise behind it.

Louise Nevelson and Jean Dubuffet have been more successful with large scale in lower Manhattan, though they too have not engaged in real collaborations here. Nevelson's *Louise Nevelson Plaza* (11), which consists of five black metal pieces in a small triangular park, is a handsome and dignified work, its tall pieces like metal trees amidst the high buildings; it is just strong enough to create a real presence here, and its scale is appropriate. The Nevelsons work best, it should be noted, against the most ornate of the several buildings which form the walls of the plaza, the mock-Strozzi Palace of the Federal Reserve Bank of New York. Here there is rich texture and a sense of brooding depth; Nevelson's works complement these qualities and enhance them.

Similarly after the fact, and at least as successful, is the immense Dubuffet *Group of Four Trees* at 1 Chase Manhattan Plaza (12). This work sits on the plaza, as opposed to Noguchi's piece below it; it was conceived more than a decade after

11

the tower was completed and can only be called a sculptor's response to a work of architecture, not a collaboration. But Dubuffet knew just what Bunshaft's skyscraper needed: he did not challenge its silver colors, but echoed them in his own neutral tones, offering instead varied texture and eccentric form. Here despite the absence of true collaboration, one senses a wholeness—the building has been vastly enriched, and it is difficult to imagine the sculpture existing so successfully anywhere else.

It is valid, then, to put such events into the category of collaborations, despite the fact that the shared effort was over time, for the artist is clearly responding to a particular architectural circumstance. Some of the recent efforts to place sculpture in public places, while laudable, are a separate issue, however, for they do not always involve even this degree of response to a specific building site. They can, however, dramatically alter our perceptions of a place—as Roy Lichtenstein was able to do with his Maillol-like outdoor sculpted figure near Miami, which turned a public open space into something approaching a piece of theater. The sculptures by Nevelson and Dubuffet that stood at the 60th Street entrance to Central Park in New York each transformed that urban gateway in its own way, making it monumentally formal in the one case, monumentally casual in the other. The Nevelson work, since moved to the middle of Park Avenue at 92nd Street, took on yet another meaning in this duller context—instead of being the formalizing element, it became the enlivening one.

The issue of public art in general is a broad one and cannot be dealt with fully here. But it should be noted that the movement toward placing art in public places, however mixed the quality of particular works or of discernment in their placement, has been a force that can only improve the climate for successful collaborations between artists and architects in general. That said, however, most public art projects have *not* been particularly noteworthy. City Walls, the large-scale murals by well-known artists in various cities sponsored by City Walls, Inc. (13–17), an organization related to the Public Art Fund, are

12

11  *Louise Nevelson,* Shadows
and Flags, *Louise Nevelson
Plaza, New York, 1978.*

12  *Jean Dubuffet,* Group of
Four Trees, *Chase Manhattan
Plaza, New York, 1972.*

13

14

*13 Tanya, Untitled, New York, 1970.*

*14 Jason Crum, Peace, New York, 1969.*

especially disappointing—most of them are just pretty pictures, blown up to vast size, and they all too rarely have indicated any real interest on the part of artists in responding to the nature of the architecture of which their work is a part. The program has given some younger artists welcome public exposure, and the murals have in many cases provided much-needed infusions of color to parts of cities that are surely in need of this, but ironically, the works themselves tend to be more attractive after they have been up for several years and their initial color has begun to fade. And the City Walls are especially disappointing where they do relate to what might be called a serious architectural context—Robert Wiegand's *Leverage*, painted on the side of the building next to Lever House in New York at 53rd Street and Park Avenue in 1970, is a weak abstraction, its forms and colors a poor foil indeed for the sharp and energetic architecture to which it is joined.

There have been some notable successes, though. The dramatic mural on the side of a building in Venice, California, showing a freeway broken off in the air as a result of an earthquake, is a powerful, if melodramatic, work, fully attuned to the spirit of the place of which it is a part. And the murals of Richard Haas (16–17), who by now has become the acknowledged master of urban trompe l'oeil, can surely be said to be deeply concerned about commenting on the architectural context. Indeed, such comment is really the sole purpose of Haas's public-scale work, from his whimsical cast-iron facade in New York's SoHo, painted onto the masonry side of a cast-iron building, to his eighteenth-century row of buildings painted onto the blank wall of a modern Edward Larrabee Barnes–designed power station in lower Manhattan near the South Street Seaport (16), to his extraordinary Renaissance trompe l'oeil on the side of the Boston Architectural Center, as sharp a comment on that building's Brutalist style as any critic could ever hope to make.

But even Haas has not succeeded totally. His Venetian Gothic wall inside the atrium of the Hyatt Regency Hotel in Cambridge, Massachusetts, by Graham Gund, is weak and decorative; the difference between the world Haas summons up

16

17

15   Mel Pekarsky, Untitled,
New York, 1970.

16   Richard Haas, Untitled,
New York, 1978.

17   Richard Haas, Untitled,
New York, 1976.

15

18

18  *Venturi, Rauch, & Scott-Brown, Western Plaza, Washington, D.C., 1980.*

and the world of Gund—an architecture of red bricks and sharp edges—is too vast, and the two aesthetics never communicate. The huge atrium is like a gulf that is never bridged.

Some good artists do respond, however, to relatively banal surroundings. Surely the excellent environmental sculptures of David von Schlegell, whose brooding, primal forms seem to have within them both the sense of acceptance of their surroundings and the air of challenge, are not diminished by ordinary architecture. Von Schlegell's stark *India Wharf Project* in Boston of 1972 at once tolerates the aesthetic of its neighbor, I. M. Pei's stark Harbor View Towers, and takes issue with it. The dialogue in any case is a more subtle one than that which Henry Moore conducts with Pei. Tony Smith's work, less brooding and more active, seems similarly able to respond to ordinary surroundings— his minimalist pieces are solids, filling the voids, both physical and conceptual, of so much contemporary architecture. (Smith is notable also in that he is among the few sculptors whose work is not compromised by its execution at a vast scale compatible with contemporary architecture.)

And occasionally when the reverse situation occurs, that of an architectural context which is not banal but which makes a powerful and articulate statement of its own, collaboration fails to work. The terminated collaboration between sculptor Richard Serra and architect Robert Venturi of Venturi, Rauch & Scott-Brown on a square for Pennsylvania Avenue in Washington, D.C. (18), is a case in point. Venturi's ideas for the square involved a pair of monumental pylons, which left no room for Serra; moreover, there was little if any common ground aesthetically on which the two men might meet.

Venturi's work, unlike, say, Bunshaft's, is strongly symbolic—it is full of allusions to history, of references to cultural traditions of buildings, and frequently enough, of ornament too. It contains little that can be called abstract—and the abstractions of an artist like Serra cannot always coexist easily with it. Though one should recall here how Venturi's installation of a major sculpture exhibition at the Whitney Museum of American Art in 1975, an elaborate, even somewhat precious,

design, did in fact try to accommodate itself to a range of different aesthetics.

The lack of hospitality that so-called Post-Modernism, as represented by Venturi and others, seems to provide to modern works is in stark contrast with the ability of modern architecture to exist as a suitable, if neutral, background for figurative sculptures. One is reminded here of Mies van der Rohe's preference for representational sculptures within his abstracted, purist spaces; he knew that they could provide scale and a proper sense of contrast with the architectural setting. This view was continued by Mies's disciple, Gene Summers, who with Phyllis Lambert renovated the Biltmore Hotel in Los Angeles in the mid-1970s; he commissioned Jim Dine to create a series of bas-reliefs and colored prints for the Miesian interiors, and the Dine pieces work superbly, providing a gentle contrast with both the original surroundings and the Miesian overlay (19).

It may be, of course, that the values that Mies's figures brought to his work are believed by the architects of the Post-Modern style to be already present in their work; surely Post-Modernism's rejection of abstraction suggests this intent on the part of the architects. But to leave it at that would be to let architecture off the hook, in a sense, and to suggest that true collaborations are not really a worthwhile goal. Surely a number of architects today do seem uncomfortable with the notion of collaboration—they seem to believe, in effect, that their works are complete and cannot in fact be improved significantly by the act of codesign with any artist. Richard Meier, himself an artist and also at the New York State Museum in Albany in 1976 the designer of one of the most sensitive installations of an exhibit of abstract art, nonetheless rarely works in close accord with any artist. Neither do Charles Gwathmey and Robert Siegel, whose works tend toward considerable abstraction, or Charles Moore, who prefers to decorate with folk art or found objects if at all, or Robert Stern, or Kevin Roche, or Cesar Pelli. With Michael Graves the problem is reversed—Graves, a painter, often uses his own work in his architecture, and if his work can be faulted at all, it is that his buildings sometimes have too painterly a quality about them, as if they were not really buildings first but three-dimensional exercises in painting. Only Frank Gehry among major contemporary architects seems really eager to work in tandem; his trapezoidal Ron Davis house in the Malibu hills of 1974 is as much a comment on that painter's work as it is a piece of architecture on its own, and one can see clearly how Davis's paintings since the house was built have picked up on cues from Gehry and taken a number of themes further. Neither artist's nor architect's work would be quite the same without their coming together here, and it is impossible, seven years later, to know precisely who contributed what, who affected whom in what way—how much the architecture made the art, how much the art made the architecture.

The Gehry-Davis collaboration may not be unique, but it is surely unusual, and its special nature makes clear the problem facing artists and architects today. Both Frank Gehry and Ron Davis were committed to the other's work. More than sympathetic onlookers to each other, they permitted their work to change in form in order to take into account the work of the other. Rarer still, it was the architect, not the artist, who was the lead force in the collaboration; Gehry did not create an architectural setting on his own and leave it up to the artist to do all the accommodating.

In general, however, the climate as of this moment is not conducive to this sort of effort. We have an attitude of respect for the notion of art and architecture in tandem, an attitude of sympathy for the idea of art within works of architecture, but little patience for true collaboration. Thus we end up not merely with the many instances of sculpture as antidote to architecture, as in the case of the much-used and much-abused Henry Moore and Alexander Calder works, but also with the phenomenon of the current fashion for setting aside a percentage of the costs of new construction as a budget for art. Such budgetary requirements are well intentioned, but they emerge out of the instinct toward juxtaposition; they do nothing to encourage true collaboration, to turn the tide back to a time when artists and architects worked together more comfortably.

Modern architecture, the pieties of the Bauhaus notwithstanding, did not welcome collaboration. Juxtaposition, as Mies demonstrated in his renderings showing classical sculpture within his purist spaces, was the goal. This was how architects could demonstrate their commitment to the "humanist values" without letting the demands of these values get in the way of the formalist priorities of their architecture. And juxtaposition has not, on balance, been a failure; the modern buildings that have been aided by the addition of works of sculpture and painting are substantial in number. But even the most successful juxtapositions do not, in the end, live up to the potential of the commingling of the artistic and the architectural imaginations—they are missed chances, so to speak, instances in which true communication has been passed by.

It is surprising that younger architects who have turned away from the Modern Movement have not also rejected the Modernist attitude toward collaboration. For all too often they see themselves, as modern architects have, as the only makers of form, as the creators of shapes and containers within which other things may be put, but which need never have their forms determined by the aesthetic of anyone but the architect. The architect as the primary creative force, a notion which the Bauhaus and all orthodox Modernism encouraged, remains, even as architects seek alternatives to the Modernist aesthetic. It will not be until that view changes that the outlook for true collaboration can be considered brighter.

*19*

*19  Jim Dine,* Four Robes Existing in a Veil of Tears, *Biltmore Hotel, Los Angeles, 1977.*

The largest single client for public art today is the United States General Services Administration (GSA), which has commissioned, in less than two decades, nearly 200 major works by almost as many artists to embellish federal facilities. While the government's role as patron was neither conceived nor planned in an orderly fashion, the growing volume of its efforts, encouraged by an impressive number of successes, suggests that what has been accomplished is only the beginning. Pending legislation (S.2080, The Public Buildings Act of 1979) allocating one-half percent of new building costs for the acquisition of art will assure its place as an integral element in future major federal construction. In light of GSA's commitment to the visual arts, the inevitable questions arise: how good a client has the government been, and what are the prospects for the future?

Government's entrance into patronage of the arts is not new. The nineteenth-century view that federal buildings symbolize the governmental presence encouraged the use of commemorative and historic art to adorn important buildings. All these efforts had the specific objective of constructing a ceremonial ambience in a particular site, which expressed the government's essential role in American society. The first major effort on a continuing basis began as an outgrowth of the economic needs of the 1930s when the Treasury Department selected both artists and their subject matter for its extensive public building programs. Between 1934 and 1943, the Treasury Department's Section of Fine Arts held 190 competitions, resulting in the award of 1,371 commissions. In addition, WPA (Works Progress Administration) monies were used to hire artists for other commissions. Across the land, murals, sculpture, and decorative forms appeared in federal buildings. Art was also commonly viewed as a way to bring New Deal ideology to citizens in an easily understood form while providing designers with gainful employment. Following an era of disdain, the work produced during those years has, over the past decade, attracted admiration in a new phase of concern with the appearance of public facilities.

World War II brought a halt to federal spending for the arts and almost two decades elapsed before GSA directed that fine arts again be incorporated in its buildings. The implementation of the GSA fine arts policy has been subject to considerable variation in intensity because of budgetary fluctuations, the interest of GSA's various administrators who have principal say in the degree of program implementation, and the imperatives of the government they serve. The program began in 1962 and, over a four-year period, realized forty-five projects. It was suspended between 1966 and 1972. It was not until 1973 that the GSA's Art-in-Architecture Program's major activity began. Since that time, more than 120 projects have been completed in some sixty federal buildings. Another twenty-five are underway in twenty buildings, while more than fifty other projects are currently being contemplated.

The range of commissions and purchases is remarkable in its overall quality and variety of style. The best of the work forms a legacy of masterful contributions to our artistic patrimony, projects that have brought the accomplishments of outstanding artists of our time within the daily experience of millions of Americans. Over all, the aim of the administrators of the Art-in-Architecture Program is to provide the public with the best work possible. Inevitably, not every work achieves the highest level; some are honest, but dull. No selection system can be devised that will assure masterpieces. Some of the program's mixed success can be attributed to its relative brevity of operation and the changing circumstances that have affected it. However, now that it is more firmly established and its continuation as a regular element in future government building is expected, a review of the program's efforts as well as a consideration of future objectives and the means contemplated for achieving them are appropriate. Addressed might be such questions as:

1. What are the successful aspects of the program: which of these should be continued, which modified for greater effectiveness, and which eliminated?
2. What are the long-term goals?
3. How can continuity be assured in achieving them?

# The Government as Patron

*By Stephen Prokopoff*

4. Are the definitions of structures and sites to be embellished and the kinds of work to be used fixed or flexible?

5. Is flexibility in the selection process required to accommodate special social and aesthetic needs? And, if so, how can it be gained?

While it is inevitable that these and similar questions will be posed, a look at the program as it now operates may yield material for future general review.

In the awarding of public contracts, selection is almost always a thorny issue. GSA, with the National Endowment for the Arts, has worked out a panel system in which respected art professionals and representatives of the community nominate artists of established national and regional reputation for each project. From a recommended list of three, provided by the panel, GSA's administrator makes a final choice. Both the quality of the lists and the choices provide ample evidence of the serious purpose and responsibility of the system. And unlike the case in many private commissions, it prevents the architect from dominating the selection. Yet, while the selection procedure is fair and successful as far as it goes, it nevertheless results in an effort that is not truly collaborative.

At present, the design of the building comes first; only later is thought given to the works of art that are expected to add significantly to the whole. Typically, the artist is selected on the basis of ability to provide the kind of work already designated. Within the context of such a procedure, art is perceived as a detail, an adornment enriching a public aspect of the building. The architect's preoccupation is with practical matters as well as his own aesthetic vision of the building; there is no compelling reason to take seriously the complexities or potential rewards in a collaboration with the artist. Rather, the creator of a mural or a sculpture is a "vendor," like so many other suppliers.

It must be said that there is little in the average architect's professional education that prepares him for collaboration with artists. Without a sharing of artistic goals, it is rarely possible to achieve the unity of vision that characterizes the major historical collaborations of art and architecture: shared expressive attitude and style, mutual concern with function—practical and symbolic—and scale. In practice, the onus in GSA commissions has been on artists to formulate solutions compatible with an extant architectural conception. The considerable history of success to date may be ascribed primarily to the abilities of artists who have managed to work within existing limitations. The limitations have been conventional, for the most part, usually focused on siting one or more large works of sculpture or painting in the public spaces in or adjacent to a federal facility. Alternatives to this formula, reflecting the very wide range of diversity in contemporary artistic production, have yet to be fully explored. Why always a large work? And why the inevitable sculpture or mural? Could not the graphic arts, photography, crafts, video, and film be integrated into the aesthetic context? Considered, too, might be ephemeral projects such as performance and other activities of a limited duration. And just as the boundaries between the arts have become blurred in recent years, why not include contributions from the performing arts as an element in the art and architecture program?

A wider perspective such as this was recommended by August Heckscher in a report on the arts prepared for President John F. Kennedy in 1962. GSA, it should be noted, is now seeking to incorporate some of these ideas into its new program. The New Federal Building in San Jose, California, for example, promises an integration of craft forms in the architectural plan. It is also expected that the artists participating in this project, all working in various craft media, will be designated shortly after the architect is appointed and that there will be a dialogue between artists and architect before the building design is begun.

Since the collaboration of architect and artist is an exchange, it is useful to suggest some of the ingredients of an ideal dialogue:

1. Art should be recognized as a presence throughout the project; this understanding must exist from the first. Art should be defined

1

1   *Alexander Calder,* Flamingo, *Chicago, 1974.*

2.   *Louise Nevelson,* Bicentennial Dawn, *Philadelphia, 1976.*

3   *Al Held,* Order/Disorder/Ascension/Descension, *Philadelphia, 1977.*

not only as the inevitable sculpture or mural—
although in some situations these will be the *right*
solutions—but also as door knobs and lighting
fixtures, as gardens and furnishings.

2. Architect and artist should be compatible
stylistically and should understand that effective
collaboration enhances the contributions of each.

3. Each project should be seen as an opportunity
to find imaginative solutions and thus contribute to
the community of which it is a part.

An important ingredient in the success of art *in*
public places is an integrating emphasis on the art
*of* public places. In the eighteenth and nineteenth
centuries, public buildings were a focus for civic
life. A means for restoring some of this sense today
is intended through the 1976 Public Buildings
Cooperative Use Act, which allows the ground
floors of federal buildings to be opened up for
commercial and cultural uses in order to combat
the deadening effects of large office buildings on
their urban context. In this spirit, the public
enthusiasm evident in such festive inaugurations as
those for Chicago's Calder or Philadelphia's
Nevelson should be extended to a continuing
ambience of educational activities, hospitality, and
distinguished decor and signage.

2

In light of the proposed criteria for an ideal art
and architecture collaboration, a glance at a
number of realized projects is in order. All these
works can be described properly as artistic
successes; and they represent only a modest part of
GSA's most successful achievements. Among these,
a few are radiant partners in a unity of artistic
object and setting. Some survive despite their
surroundings; and still others are virtually lost in
an overwhelming built context.

Alexander Calder's *Flamingo* (1) of 1974 is one of
GSA's triumphs. The red stabile, its fluid contours
a rich contrast to the sober, handsome facade of
the Federal Building, animates the Federal Plaza
in Chicago. A superb ensemble, it forms one of the
most inviting and well-used public spaces in the
Loop.

*Bicentennial Dawn* (2) of 1976, Louise Nevelson's
constellation of inventively designed white totems,
magically illuminated, fills the foyer of this

3

4

5

6

4 *Stephen Antonakos*, Red Neon Circle Fragments on a Blue Wall, *Dayton, Ohio, 1978.*

5 *Charles Ross*, Origin of Colors, *Lincoln, Nebraska, 1976.*

6 *Lenore Tawney*, Cloud Series, *Santa Rosa, California, 1978.*

7 *George Sugarman*, Baltimore Federal, *Baltimore, 1978.*

conventional Philadelphia office building, the U.S. Courthouse, with fantasy and great dignity.

The ambiguous geometry of Al Held's black and white mural *Order/Disorder/Ascension/Descension* (3) of 1977 in Philadelphia's Social Security Administration Building produces, with very different means, a kindred sense of order, complexity, and subtle wit to that found in Nevelson's work. Held's eccentric geometry plays off the regularity of its architectural surroundings in a particularly imaginative counterpoint.

The fluent geometry of Stephen Antonakos's *Red Neon Circle Fragments on a Blue Wall* (4) of 1978, articulated by neon elements, enlivens the simplicity of the Federal Building in Dayton, Ohio. The arabesque is, of course, particularly handsome at night when its luminous dance alludes to the bright play of city lights.

Charles Ross's *Origin of Colors* (5) of 1976 is one of the most innovative of GSA's successes, especially so because it engaged an artist who works with such an unconventional material as reflected light. Ross's work floods a mezzanine and staircase in Lincoln, Nebraska, with carefully balanced patterns of rainbow light.

Lenore Tawney's *Cloud Series* (6) of 1978 is a very different kind of light play from Ross's, although, like his, it is one based on natural phenomena. Here, poetic showers of thousands of strands of light-catching linen threads, each individually dyed and painted, mitigate the heavy austerity of a typical corporate-style building in Santa Rosa, California.

George Sugarman's vivacious, brightly colored *Baltimore Federal* (7) of 1978 in Baltimore was, among a few of GSA's commissions, the subject of considerable public controversy. This seems surprising for such an amiable work, one that immediately invites the public to move through it or to sit and enjoy its ambience. *Baltimore Federal* does much to enliven the conventionally sturdy office building that is its foil.

Chicago's *Batcolumn* (8) of 1977 by Claes Oldenburg, at once whimsical and strangely monumental, quickly assumed the character of a city emblem. The ordinary building that it fronts has the virtue of a mirror facade that reflects the

7

8

masterwork.

The pensive evocation of ordinary life in George Segal's *The Restaurant* (9) of 1976, in which three bronze figures subtly express the alienation that is so persistent an aspect of our time, is obscured by the unremitting visual clamor of the modular facade of the Federal Building in Buffalo, New York, that is the background for this beautiful work.

A dramatic example of incompatibility can be seen in the combination of Isamu Noguchi's lovely *Landscape of Time* (10) of 1975 and the Federal Office Building in Seattle, Washington. The artist's quietist conception of a garden of stones arranged in graceful relationships is overwhelmed by the massiveness of its otherwise handsome architectural setting.

How can one not be delighted by Jack Beal's four murals *The History of Labor in America* (11) of 1977 in the Department of Labor Building in Washington, D.C.? Beal revives an earlier mural tradition, the kind that decorated major public buildings at the turn of the century. With splendid, knowing, historical relish, the artist evokes the idealizing formulas of an earlier day in a superb work for the present.

And, finally, Ned Smyth, in *Reverent Grove* (12) of 1978, brings together another set of conventions, those of a stylish 1930s tropicality. These form an elegant, beautifully decorative work that is imaginatively and wittily in accord with its Virgin Islands setting.

In considering GSA's projects, scale emerges as a crucial factor. The best collaborations are those in which the work of art is able to affect and articulate its surrounding space. In practice—and not surprisingly—this has meant interior spaces. The particular effectiveness of the works by Held, Nevelson, Ross, and Smyth is enormously enhanced by the visual ambience they create within the architectural setting and the complexity of the dialogue established with the site.

Exterior spaces, especially when they are shaped and dominated by the massive forms of highrises, often overwhelm even the largest and most vibrant sculptural works. Calder's *Flamingo* succeeds less as a relatively small and brilliant contrast to the Federal Building's regular facade than because it

9

8  *Claes Oldenberg*, Batcolumn,
*Chicago, 1977.*

9  *George Segal*, The Restaurant, *Buffalo, 1976.*

10

12

animates the "room" space created by the cluster of buildings surrounding its plaza. Oldenburg's *Batcolumn* is fortunate in being poised before a reflective facade that allows the column to assert its presence.

Appropriateness of architecture to the work of art is another factor in achieving visual unity. Again, in the projects surveyed, this is best attained indoors, although Antonakos's luminous neon fragments offer a handsome exception. The Segal and Noguchi commissions provide examples in which architectural forms are inimical to the artists' conceptions.

While it is difficult to fault the GSA's seriousness in seeking to find beautiful and significant works of art, it is clear that integration into the site has not always been sensitively considered. However, it is also true that the architecture commissioned by GSA is considerably below the level of its artistic choices.

Some of the problems of the Art-in-Architecture Program are endemic in a society that perceives art as a detail. This view is exacerbated in the context of public expenditure, which is appropriately subject to scrutiny. Without legislative authority, the GSA program is particularly vulnerable to criticism and to the vagaries of inadequate staffing and ad hoc planning. Yet, the potential for splendid accomplishments remains. Congressional support will provide the legitimacy and stability needed for an increasingly innovative civic encounter between art and architecture.

11

10  *Isamu Noguchi*, The Landscape
of Time, *Seattle, 1975.*

11  *Jack Beal*, The History of
Labor in America, *Washington,
D.C., 1977.*

12  *Ned Smyth*, Reverent
Grove, *Virgin Islands, 1978.*

# Part 3

# The Future

We are all familiar with the equestrian statues on the war memorials or the allegorical mural paintings of thrift, commerce, and industry at the local bank, legacies of the time when artists and architects were trying to revive traditional relationships among the fine arts. Sometimes these efforts at integration of the arts were successful, particularly in churches and important public buildings; but, even at their best, they tend to recall Richard Norman Shaw's rueful verdict on the products of revivalism in the arts: "like cut flowers, beautiful but dead."

We are also familiar with the results of the Bauhaus initiative; too often all the arts have in common is the lowest common denominator. Even when the best artists and architects were involved, the ideas that found expression tended to emphasize those aspects of painting and sculpture that were closest to architecture, thus promoting the dominance of the architect. If art is the manipulation of planes and masses, or form and color, reasoned the architect, why couldn't the architect do all that—why involve another artist? To put the question another way, if a sculptor is going to create a composition of painted pipes out on the plaza, why shouldn't the architect paint the pipes that were already part of the architecture?

Now artists and architects are looking beyond the Bauhaus, both back to the Beaux-Arts and forward to some as yet only dimly perceived form of expression. The Art Moderne work done from the 1920s through the 1940s is looking less and less like a failed compromise and more like a promising point of departure. At this interesting moment there might be some new means of collaboration among architects and other artists.

As part of our Centennial project, The Architectural League determined to try an experiment. We would commission a series of collaborations, hoping that we would be shown ways of giving new life to old traditions as well as perhaps discovering modes of collaboration that had not been tried before.

I believe our experiment has indeed been successful; the results are valuable in them-selves and suggest directions for the future.

Before we try to interpret the results, however, it is important to understand the context in which our commissions were carried out.

## Our Frame of Reference

Obviously The League could not commission actual structures, so we asked the architects and artists involved to select a subject that was of interest to them and relevant to the problems of the decade ahead. We suggested that their choice be visionary, but, at the same time, realizable. The commissions thus did not necessarily include the constraints, both utilitarian and financial, which are embodied in an actual situation. If these disciplines are visible in the work, it is because the collaborators brought them to the problem themselves or because our curator, Barbaralee Diamonstein, has been able to encourage them to think along these lines.

The League was able to offer the architects and artists a respectable honorarium, but it does not begin to compare with the fees involved in a real building project. Some have taken our commission as a reason for investigating a specific situation in detail and have ended by contributing a large amount of time and material. They have also had to take time away from other, more real commissions. Others of the collaborators chose to present polemic rather than projects, producing results that are equally interesting in a different way.

The selection of participants certainly could not be definitive; economic and space restrictions limited the numbers involved. We have been agreeably surprised by how many eminent architects and artists expressed interest in participating in this project; and we wish we could have included them all.

The League has selected the architects; and the architects in their turn were asked to select the artists (subject to our approval) because this is the way that participants in building design are chosen. There are two exceptions, which came about in the following way. Originally, Alice Aycock, a sculptor whose work is considered to have an architectural character, and Michael Graves, an architect whose work has been called painterly, were chosen by The League to do complete projects on their own. You might say that their projects were to be a "control" for our experiment in collaboration. At

# Beyond Revivalism and the Bauhaus: A New Partnership in the Arts

*By Jonathan Barnett*

one of the meetings that the curator held with the participants, another architect, who is himself a painter, protested that everyone involved should be working in a similar way. After considering this request, Alice Aycock and Michael Graves generously agreed to do so. Alice Aycock chose architect James Ingo Freed as her collaborator and Michael Graves invited painter Lennart Anderson to work with him.

## Three Categories of Result
The projects seem to fall into three categories. The first group is a series of variations on the traditional relationships between architect and painter or between architect and sculptor. Of the four projects in this category, two are buildings that could be constructed tomorrow if someone were prepared to pay for them, and two, while they could be built, are really illustrations for a polemic.

A second group tries to create a new relationship between architect and artist, one in which the work of the artist and the architect is more equal than is traditional, and where there is less of a separation between building and work of art. Two of these projects have been created around situations where the usual functional complexities of architecture did not apply. In the third, which is a far more ambitious and complicated proposal, the architect and artist have ended by disagreeing in a way that throws an interesting light on the problems of collaboration.

The third group, which represents an unexpected result to our experiment, might be called "visions of the city." The artist and architect have collaborated on a concept for some aspect of the city. Neither the architect nor the artist is playing an accustomed role, and the collaboration is on the idea itself rather than on individual elements of the project. Again the proposals range from the practical to the polemical; and there is another interesting and instructive dispute between one set of collaborators.

## Variations of the Traditional Theme
The firm of Hardy Holzman Pfeiffer has devised a situation which, while it is not a real project, could easily become one. Bryant Park, in the heart of New York City's midtown business district, is surely a viable location for the restaurant they propose. A cogent argument can be made that the use of part of a public park in this way will actually make the whole park more accessible, as the subculture that has taken over much of Bryant Park frightens many people away.

The concept proposed and the nature of the collaboration are both very much in the tradition of the American Renaissance. The neighboring New York Public Library is a masterpiece of that tradition; and Bryant Park was redesigned to harmonize with the Public Library during the 1930s—interestingly enough as the result of a competition sponsored by The Architectural League. Bryant Park has the strong axial composition and symmetry of a formal garden, as well as the terraces, stairways, and balustrades of formal garden architecture.

The proposed restaurant is designed around an existing fountain on the main axis of the library, and it has the mirror-image formality that is traditional in such a setting. The Roccoco pillars proposed by Jack Beal are equally traditional; they could almost have come out of an eighteenth-century pattern book. Beal's patterns for the colored glass roof and for carpets and walkways are part of the design of the building, reflecting a relationship between architect and artist that would have seemed axiomatic to the founders of The Architectural League one hundred years ago. Sondra Freckelton's mural paintings also reflect such a customary relationship. This project shows that the methods of collaboration used during the American Renaissance are relevant to at least some kinds of modern situations. At the same time, the art and architecture, while evocative of traditional forms, have a wit and style of their own.

The collaboration between Richard Meier and Frank Stella also reflects a traditional working relationship, but, in this case, one that does not evoke Renaissance forms. What we see are the four elevations of a characteristic Richard Meier house. Inside the windows are solar control devices of acrylic in different translucent colors that follow patterns derived from French curves. These translucent paints can be rolled up and down like the familiar cloth window shades. This concept is responsive to the needs of the occupants, who can dwell in colorful twilight, enjoy a normal view, or adopt various choices in between.

This discovery of a modern equivalent for stained glass has extensive possibilities, but is used here in a very disciplined way. The French curves are elegant found objects, if their use as the pattern for the windows requires their arrangement within a series of openings determined by the geometry of the building. The windows are thus another kind of found object, and the result is an exceptionally rigid set of constraints for the artist. On this occasion collaboration seems to have restricted the artist's options, not opened them up.

An ironic commentary on both traditional modes of collaboration and historical architecture and sculpture is offered by architect Charles Moore and sculptor Alice Atkinson (who has started calling herself Alice Wingwall for this occasion).

Stratford, the Lee family's great Virginia house that was completed about 1730, is held up as an ideal; but, as it is "not affordable" today, Stratford "fragments" are proposed instead.

Of course, the point of Stratford is that it is complete, solid, and balanced; that it approximates Alberti's ideal for a work of art: an entity to which nothing should be added and nothing taken away. The idea of Stratford fragments is a mischievous notion, something like a disco performance of Handel's *Messiah*.

Instead of the idealized human form presented without clothes, Alice Wingwall gives us clothes without the human form, another unsettling idea. A sculptural group of T–shirts and dungarees is shown atop a colonnade in attitudes reminiscent of the sculpture fragments from the pediments of the Parthenon that are part of the famous Elgin Marbles. Other T-shirts are shown on top of columns, approximately where one would expect the straining torso of a sculpted figure to be holding up the cornice.

What is the connection to Stratford, which has no such colossal sculpture, clothed or unclothed? And what is the meaning of the porchbus, which looks like a cross between movable airline stairs and the automobiles that Frank Lloyd Wright designed for Broadacre City?

What I would like to think Charles Moore and Alice Wingwall are telling us is that they hope, through homeopathic doses of Stratford, to cure the American addiction to automobiles and mobile homes, gradually returning us to an environment of stability and balance. In the meantime, the human figure can steal back into art, assuming the clothes already provided for it. So it is possible to read this project as a plea for the return of a more traditional art and architecture and a more traditional relationship between architect and artist, all expressed in a rueful and ironic way that admits that today's society is unlikely to seek Stratfords or Parthenons. However, by giving us a glossary as a statement, the authors allow us to construct all kinds of other interpretations. In the meantime, they have retired—safe in their armor of irony—to let you make of this project what you will.

A somewhat similar juxtaposition of classic themes and fragmentary architecture can be seen in the proposal by Robert Stern and Robert Graham. Graham has drawn a project for a statue and Stern has provided a pedestal. So far I might be talking about Augustus Saint-Gaudens working with McKim, Mead, & White. The Graham statue is to be a female figure cast in bronze, a classic concept although hardly a classic pose. But Stern's pedestal is actually a column, transforming the woman into a conqueror: Trajan or Lord Nelson. But wait a minute, the column is only a half circle, slanting into a series of equivocal forms vaguely reminiscent of an office building designed to fit an old-fashioned set of zoning regulations. We are told that the materials are to be "faux marble" and mirror glass. Mirror glass? Isn't that usually the skin for office buildings? How big is this thing going to be anyway: ten feet tall, the size of the Statue of Liberty, as tall as the Empire State Building? What are we to make of all this?

We see an intriguing composition, beautifully presented, and are then informed by the collaborators that it is an allegory symbolizing the current state of architecture, where Modernism and Classicism "co-exist in uneasy proximity."

When the artist tells you to interpret the work as allegory and then tells you the interpretation, that has to be the end of the matter. There is about as much room for argument as when a psychiatrist tells a patient that the patient's refusal to accept an explanation of his behavior comes from a "resistance" to the explanation. This proposal, in its very accomplished way, contains many levels of allusion and paradox. It would have been interesting to speculate about other meanings, but we must believe what we are told.

## New Modes of Collaboration

Cesar Pelli and William Bailey have sought to divide design responsibility equally. They have succeeded by downplaying those aspects of architecture that make it a profession, a science, and a business and concentrating on architecture as an art. They have created a single, private room which has none of the complexities of multiple functions or public use. The room might be a meditation chamber. It might be a separate structure, a part of a larger building, or it could exist in various settings which are demonstrated by means of collage. The adaptability of this room to different contexts is reminiscent of one of the garden structures that is derived from Bramante's Tempietto at S. Pietro in Montorio; but the point here is the internal space, not the exterior mass.

The collaborators evidently have a clear idea of what they are trying to do and are able to translate their ideas into clear and direct prose, describing such matters as the way in which they have created a continuity between the room and Bailey's paintings, which are placed within it, by designing the lighting of the room to harmonize with the light depicted in the paintings.

The collaboration between Michael Graves and Lennart Anderson also emphasizes architecture as an art rather than architecture as a means of housing various social activities. The theme is a bacchanal—not the setting for a bacchanal but a representation of a bacchanal. Michael Graves's architectural composition is an extension of the painting at the same time that it locates the painting in space and provides an organizational framework for it. The effect is reminiscent of the

integration of painted backgrounds, sculpture, and architectural vignettes in the shrines of the Sacro Monte at Varallo, which were described with such enthusiasm by Samuel Butler in *Ex Voto*—but without the same literalness. The extension of architecture into painting and of painting into architecture was an important theme in Baroque art. Why should it not be so again?

Susana Torre and Charles Simonds have undertaken to collaborate in a far more complex project, the restoration and adaptive reuse of Ellis Island in New York Harbor. The idea was that architect and artist would collaborate on the concept for the whole project rather than confining the artist's role to the one percent, or the half of one percent, that might be allocated for art. An excellent choice of subject, but one that has proved difficult to carry out. The problem, as might be expected, is that artists are not used to dealing with complicated functional issues as part of the conceptual process, while architects are not used to deferring to another sensibility while creating a design, although architects expect to make changes as required by clients and routinely take the advice of other design professionals on such matters as engineering and landscape architecture.

Charles Simonds has often worked with miniature landscapes, and by participating in the redesign of Ellis Island he has had an opportunity to work on a problem in which landscape is a major factor. The artist and architect did work together on the reorganization of the buildings that strips them to a more classical composition and on the basic rearrangement of land and levels. However, after the conceptual process was completed, Charles Simonds withdrew, and what you see are drawings and designs that are essentially the work of Susana Torre.

## Visions of the City

The vision of the city presented by Emilio Ambasz and Michael Meritet is akin to those of the City Beautiful Movement, which was an element of the American Renaissance. The whole concept is also a delicate compliment to J. Irwin Miller, who has been the patron for so much architecture and art in his home city of Columbus, Indiana. The Ambasz/

Meritet design presents Columbus as if it were the city of a Renaissance prince, a city like Florence, Italy, with an edge and gateways. The beautiful aerial map gives the important buildings of Columbus a much greater legibility than they have in reality, and the landscaped gateways would indeed enhance the sense of arrival or departure from the city.

When an architect and an artist collaborate on a vision of a city, which (to put it mildly) is not under the direct artistic control of either collaborator, how do we assess the nature of their collaboration?

According to the text submitted by the authors, the concept is by Ambasz and the realization of the images by Meritet. If this were a conventional building project, we might say that Meritet has only functioned as an illustrator, and thus we have not seen a true collaboration. However, we are talking about a visionary concept, where the illustration is the primary reality, so the illustrator does become a partner in the collaboration.

There is more than a little bit of black humor in Alice Aycock and James Freed's vision of the city. Freed postulates that in some long-ago, now-forgotten culture, what is now Times Square was considered the Omphalos, the navel of the universe. (Times Square is often described as representing various other anatomical elements of the universe.) Today only fragments of an ancient religious structure remain, segmented by Broadway and Seventh Avenue, much the way streets in modern Rome may go through the site of ancient monuments.

Alice Aycock then imagines that this ancient structure has been modified to become a "Palace of Versailles Waterworks." What takes place at the waterworks she has designed is a happening (remember when happenings were the latest works of art?), which is based on the normal bustle and low-life activities of Times Square but emphasizes the futility of much of the activity and the cruelty and sadism of many Times Square denizens.

Louise Nevelson has said that she regards New York City as an enormous sculpture. Others have taken this found-object sensibility further and have seen various events as process art. Once you have been educated to recognize found objects and process art, it is possible to regard every place and every event as some form of artistic expression. Alice Aycock and James Freed have imposed their own form and events on Times Square, but it would appear that their real intention is satiric: they have given us a new way of looking at this famous place and the events that go in it.

Frank Gehry and Richard Serra are not being satiric, but it is hard for me to understand the significance of their vision. Both have worked with industrial materials, and it seemed likely that their collaboration would produce something strong and tough-minded. A bridge is an interesting subject for a collaboration, as it might be taken as a symbol for collaboration itself. This bridge, however, appears to be a vague, utopian proposal for a connection between the top of the Chrysler Building and the World Trade Towers, or the tops of any tall office buildings. If we are meant to take the suggestion at all literally, it is a very old-fashioned kind of futurism, without any of the detail that we have come to expect in visionary proposals. The elevated roadways in the famous drawing from *King's Views of New York*, or Yona Friedman's space-frame cities that bridge over existing buildings, are presented in ways that deal systematically with the implications of such ideas. They may not be practical, but they are plausible.

If a distinguished artist and an equally distinguished architect decide to have a vision about a bridge, which is also a vision about a city, don't they have an obligation to develop the idea in more detail? Why does the bridge make this connection, what happens down below, how do you prevent the structure from pulling down the buildings it connects, and so on?

The fourth of these visions of the city concerns the city of the dead. Stanley Tigerman, the architect, has selected Richard Haas as his artist collaborator and the two have chosen the topic, "The Great American Cemetery," perhaps in contradistinction to Aldo Rossi's well-known cemetery project.

In other projects Tigerman has shown an interest

in presenting a banal suburban house as an American Icon. Here miniature suburban houses become grave markers, emphasizing the fact that many cemeteries are laid out as miniature cities and that their planning concepts derive from the same sources as those for cities and suburbs.

The collaboration between artist and architect has really been in the presentation of the idea for the exhibition: Haas's skyline painting and the Tigerman office's models create the illusions in a "box within a box."

Is this an appropriate role for an artist collaborator? Evidently Richard Haas didn't think so. He went off and selected a new collaborator, one not commissioned by The Architectural League, Edward Mills, with whom he had worked on previous projects. The necropolis that Richard Haas and Edward Mills designed bears a disturbing resemblance to the Renaissance Center office, hotel, and shopping complex in Detroit. It can be considered a perfectly serious urban design proposal, however, in a plausible location, with a carefully worked-out symbolism. It might even be financially feasible. One can envision a real-estate marketability study which determines that the project is economically viable at a purchase price of $x$ dollars a unit and an "absorption rate" of $y$ hundred a year. The obvious intent of this proposal is to present a completely different way of thinking about cemeteries from the one shown in the original concept.

**What Does It All Mean?**
Hardy Holzman Pfeiffer with Jack Beal and Sondra Freckelton have shown us that there are still opportunities for traditional modes of collaboration. Richard Meier and Frank Stella have shown us that it is not necessary to revive the medieval craft of stained glass when there are modern acrylics (not to mention roller shades) at the artist's disposal. Charles Moore, who has done so much to open the eyes of architects to the architecture the Bauhaus rejected, has collaborated with Alice Wingwall to suggest that there are also possibilities in the sculpture the Bauhaus rejected.

Cesar Pelli and Michael Graves have each

shown us different ways of bringing architecture closer to painting and to sculpture. Interestingly, they have both chosen to work with painters who depict representational forms and create illusions of space: William Bailey and Lennart Anderson.

We have also seen artists and architects collaborate on visions of the city where both are free from their customary patterns of work, and the nature of the collaboration can be completely new.

We have also seen conflicts develop between the collaborators in two of the projects, which is much less than might have been expected. In both cases the projects have been ambitious ones where the artist was to have a major role in the basic concept. The principle that the artist need not be confined to the one percent, or half percent, of a large and complex project that is allocated to art is an important one. It has worked well in several of our examples, but both architects and artists need to develop more experience of the give and take required by such collaboration.

I think we should be encouraged by this evidence that collaboration between architects and artists is not a dead academic idea, or a matter of seeking the simplest common denominator, but a vital process capable of diverse, and significant, results. Obviously, we have not heard the last word on the subject of collaboration in the arts, but we have heard some of the first new and serious words to be said in a long time.

## History

Bryant Park in its present state is neither what its numerous designers intended nor what it will become. Having served as a battlefield in the Revolution, it was set aside as a potter's field to bury the city's impoverished in 1822. Reinterment was arranged prior to 1842 when the Croton Reservoir was completed on the eastern portion to serve the rapidly expanding city. In 1853 the Crystal Palace Exhibition was set up on the park site, which at that time was designated Reservoir Square. Although a financial failure, this structure (and its spectacular eradication by fire in 1858) again claimed the site for public use. In 1884 the park was renamed for William Cullen Bryant.

The reservoir was razed in 1901, and by 1911 Carrère and Hastings' New York Public Library was completed, placing a monumental Beaux-Arts facade before Fifth Avenue and a sturdily utilitarian rear wall facing west. That same year a statue of Bryant was erected behind the library. This park was intended to give permanent recognition to America's great nineteenth-century poet, editor, and park polemicist, a man whose writing was instrumental in fostering the climate of opinion which led to the creation of Central Park. It is therefore appropriate to find his statue both in a park and next to a library. The other axial monument of the park, Lowell Fountain (relocated in 1934 to its present position on a terrace overlooking Sixth Avenue), was dedicated to Josephine Shaw Lowell in 1913. New York's first monument to a woman saluted a life of social work. Its symbolism of the refreshing and purifying effects of water is fitting testimony to her goals of social improvement.

## Present Design

Bryant Park was intended as a preserve, an oasis from city streets. It originally included "flower beds designed to obtain the best effect of massed plants and colors." To quote advocates for the park:

"The desirability of such a botanical center in the very heart of the city cannot be overestimated, either for its educational or for its aesthetic value."

In the ensuing years misuse and negligence resulted in gradual deterioration. The existing design results from a competition sponsored by The Architectural League with the dual intention of removing a public eyesore and providing work for architects during the depression. To quote a supporter of this transformation:

"With the passage of recent years this historic site that should be a national shrine, descended to become the rendezvous of the degenerate, the seller of dope, the procurer, the pickpocket, and the unfortunate jetsam and flotsam of a heterogeneous cosmopolitan metropolis."

In 1934 the Parks Department under the direction of Robert Moses shaped the site to its present configuration for passive enjoyment of nature in accordance with a design by Lusby Simpson.

The park's raised terraces, ivy beds, cottonwood trees, and formal geometric order are all intended to reinforce the axial symmetry of the Public Library with a simple and well-controlled statement. This is an ordered and contained outdoor room quite unlike the vast rolling romanticism of Central Park.

But despite this civic improvement, it is now again controlled by occupants and activities startlingly similar to those so graphically described fifty years ago.

## Park Purpose

Parks preserve land for public good at the expense of private gain. They are interruptions in the patterns of development which characterize American cities, interruptions supported by the public purse. Small parks such as Bryant Park are protected from physical encroachment by buildings, but they are so intimately tied to life in the street that changing social patterns are a direct influence on their environment. Parks reflect varied social behavior as much as they do the four seasons. Imbalances which appear in nature are no less common in human behavior (the ultimate test of both being survival).

We believe the continued well-being of Bryant Park requires uses more in keeping with its current design rather than a further transformation.

# Restaurant Pavilions for Bryant Park: Musings on Variety

*Hugh Hardy*
*with Malcolm Holzman and Norman Pfeiffer*

*Jack Beal/Sondra Freckelton*

## Proposal

Changing the social structure of the park is not possible with architecture alone (as previous reconstructions show), but we hope to at least call attention to the misuse of a prime urban resource. Our present design therefore stems from interest in a collaboration among architects and artists which could take place in a park setting and reflect the change and variety of nature. Nature's work is accomplished because of variety, and her slow and patient evolution of survival succeeds because of the presence of multiple forms of life. Parks offer an opportunity to come in contact with this profusion. We have therefore assumed construction of two new park pavilions for the pleasure of eating, thereby proposing reclamation of park space for civilizing behavior. We see these pavilions offering diversified fare within their enclosures so that picnics and specialized dining are as possible as quick snacks.

The pavilions are intended to bring people to the park in a structured way, stemming from the formal order already in place. An attraction both night and day, they would allow a more rational use of space designed for public enjoyment, permitting controlled activity to join Sixth Avenue with the park.

The opportunity to jointly explore the imagery of these park pavilions with Jack Beal and Sondra Freckelton permits us to integrate changing aspects of nature with the fixed necessities of architecture. Seen as an extension and intensification of the park, these pavilions also juxtapose two architectural vocabularies to ensure that the result avoids being static.

Jack Beal's surface patterns represent design elements found in the park. Overhead his colored glass ceilings recall seasonal foliage and underfoot his carpet designs reflect textures and materials of the walkways that border and intersect the landscape. These same designs are continued outdoors in actual masonry materials.

Jack's fanciful ceramic columns are used in a pergola sheltering the Lowell Fountain and inside as freestanding sculpture. His place settings come from the vegetable kingdom and indicate the type of small-scale detail which could personalize the eating experience.

Sondra's cartoon for one of her seasonal wall murals is included, together with a detailed watercolor of one portion of the finished work. This basket of plants celebrates the fecundity of nature, showing the full cycle of the fruit-bearing process from winter hibernation to fall harvest. It also indicates how nature's cycle of the seasons has been compressed for city dwellers, making almost everything available at once.

## Conclusion

Much as parks are supposed to provide a varied release from the mechanical sameness of urban life, restaurants offer release from its routine. New York has dining peaks and cachet interiors, but no great rooms which join the illusions of husbanded nature with those of culinary care.

This project offers a sketch of the diverse elements which might combine to make eating a pleasure. No other human activity so intimately combines people and the sustenance of nature. Eating out can make this physical necessity special and can create an intensified awareness of the shapes, colors, textures, and patterns of food.

This project *suggests* a building rather than defining one. It places together sculptural and decorative elements drawn from the park and its environs. It offers the opportunity for a collaboration of artists and architects similar to those which produced the city's public rooms in the past. Although the project is not complete in organization and detail, we have nonetheless put together an impression of the type of juxtaposition and celebration of seasonal variety we admire.

## Media

The architectural design is presented as a collage of Xeroxed materials based on both drawings and photographs. Graphic coordinations: Donald Billinkoff and David Mohney.

The artwork is in watercolor.

FIFTH AVENUE

AVENUE OF THE AMERICAS

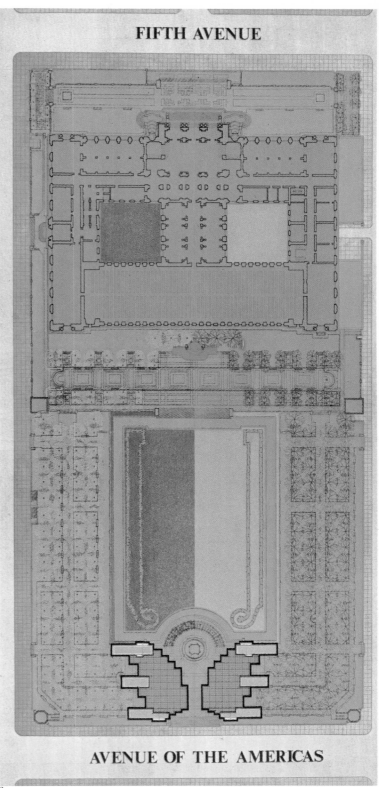

3

1 Sixth Avenue elevation.

2 Elevation from park.

3 Site plan.

4

5

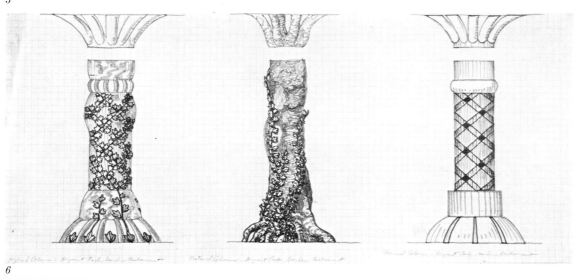

6

7

8

9

10

7 *Carpet patterns.*

8 *Paving patterns.*

9 *Carpet detail.*

10 *Garden view detail.*

The art decorations for this house, which is a typical one-family suburban residence, exist in all glazed areas. The designs for all the window openings consist of aluminum foil outlines on tinted mylar window shades, which serve both as inexpensive architectural decoration and as protection from the sun.

Although this house was originally planned for a specific client and site, this collaboration shows one way in which the architect and the artist can work together without getting in each other's way. Architecture can be structurally free from decoration and yet have decorative potential. One is not committed to a permanent and fixed architectural decoration. Here the applied decoration is temporary and can easily be modified to suit the critical taste of the times.

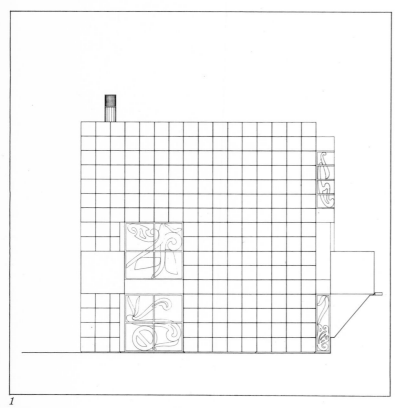

1

# Tinted Shades

*By Richard Meier and Frank Stella*

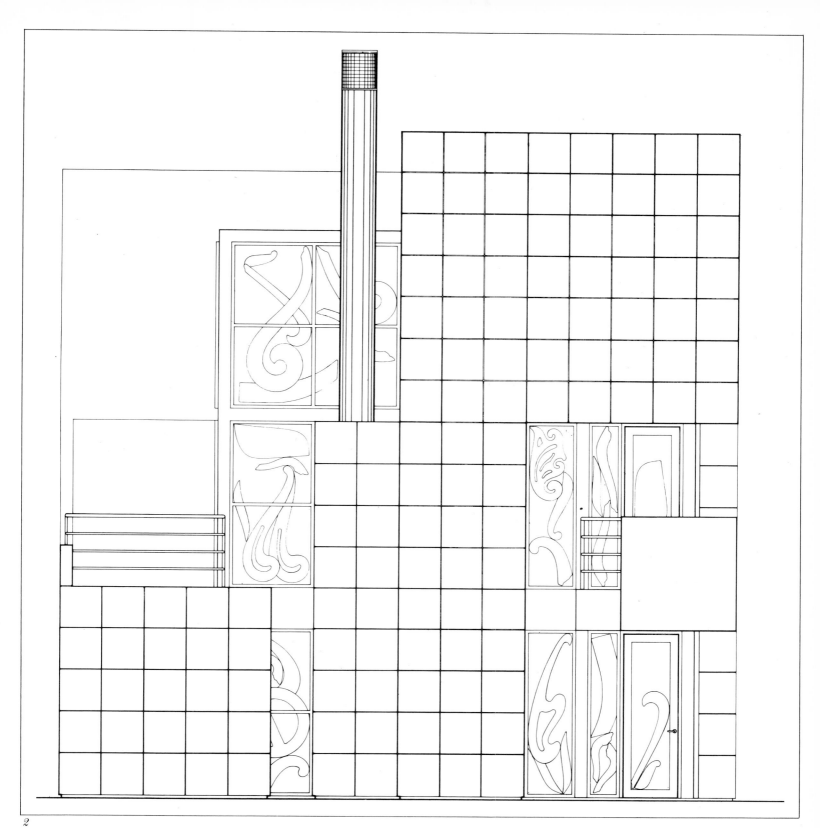

2

1  *North elevation.*

2  *East elevation.*

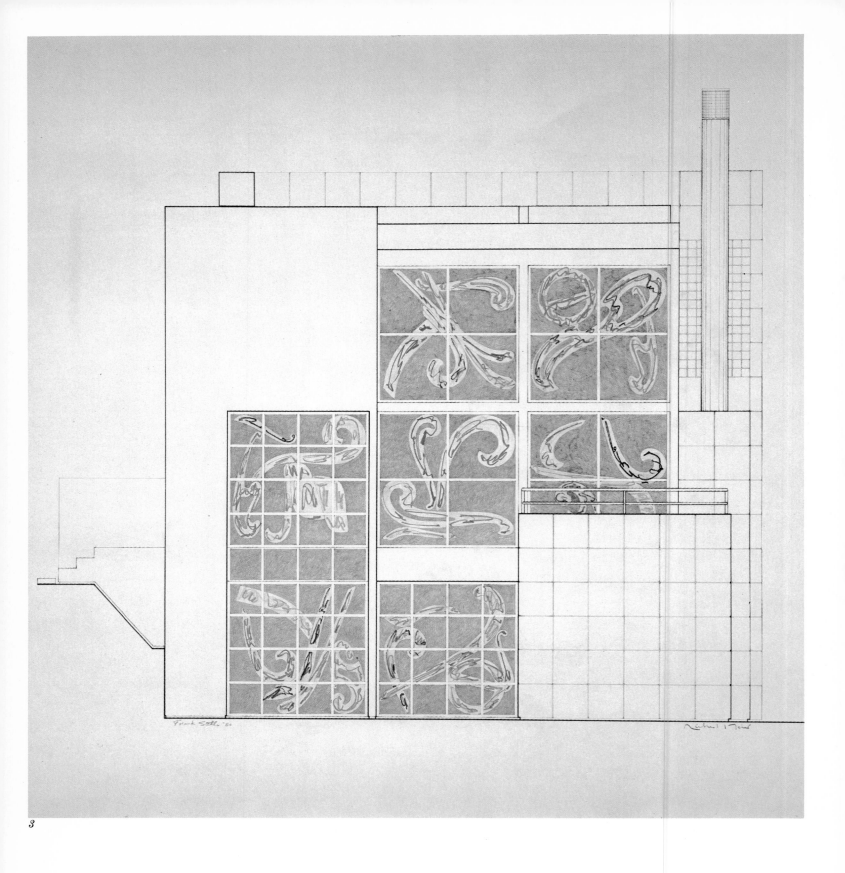

3

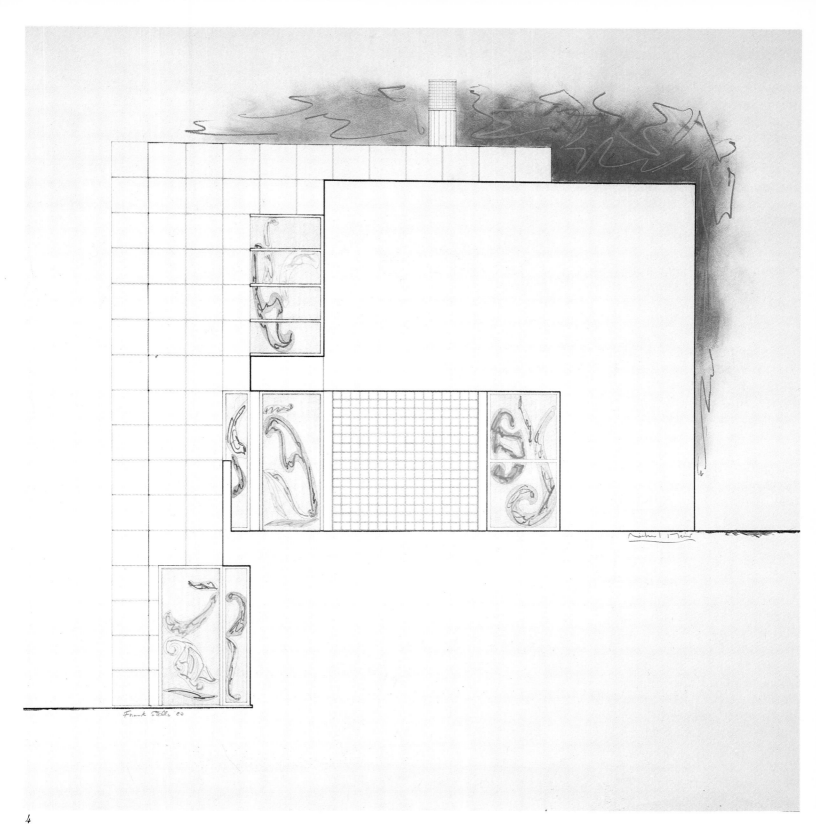

4

3   *South elevation.*

4   *West elevation.*

## Glossary

**Articulated Components:** House fragment with grand mirrored stairway, two porticoes surmounted by heroic gestures, and various porchbuses.

**Blue Jeans, Coveralls:** Monuments in the new gestural order working atop buildings.

**Building Blocks:** Movable spatial enclosures.

**Courtyard:** Changeable by portico position.

**Domain:** Landed property which one has in his/her own right. May be fenced in or defined by porticoes.

**Figurative Sculpture:** Making a comeback. Thigh in the sky.

**Fragment:** A small detached portion, an incomplete part that can be reconstructed. A remnant which can be new.

**Future:** On its way, but not quite here yet. It surely includes the return of figure sculpture, but quite properly advocating a gradualist approach, we mean to start with the blue jeans, coveralls, and T-shirts, expecting the arrival of the fleshier parts in due time. Higher-tech items such as holographic spaces and *Dial-a-Spandrel* are in another segment of the future, labeled *Later.*

**Gesture:** Mode of action; the position or attitude of the body; motions of the body or its limbs, or their surrogates, as a means of expression. May be formal or courteous; deliberate, symbolic, or notable.

**Heroic:** Elevated to the roof, looming large in legend and in bronze.

**Loading Dock:** Elevated main entrance to the house, the heroic entrance. The base of the grand stairway.

**Mag Wheels:** Found on porticoes and porchbuses, affording an extendable domain.

**Memory:** Image recall of many beloved dwellings.

**Movable:** Everything except the triangular house fragment, allowing redefinition and recombination of the domain and its parts.

**Pedestal:** Elevates gestures.

**Pediment:** Suggested by massed heroic gestures that recall their architectural and sculptural ancestors.

**Porch:** Covered entrance associated with a door or gate. Smaller house in front of a bigger house. Can be a shadowy zone of demarcation between a house and a plaza, or a house and a meadow, or a house and a house.

**Porchbus:** A projectile porch giving access to the loading dock and to the exterior of the property. A room on wheels recalling some original house. A pedestal for sculptures.

**Portal:** A city gate, a porch, a door, a gate, an entrance, particularly a grand or imposing one with a roof. A gathering place. A constructed memory of an *allée.*

**Portico:** Colonnade, possibly covered, at the entrances to buildings.

**Revision:** The elephant remains to be seen.

**Site:** A tiny portion of the surface of the planet earth controlled by the client and therefore favored by him for the installation of his project. The architect and artist have no control over this.

**Stair:** Mirrored. Connects the loading dock to the window of appearances. Smaller, nonmirrored versions found on porchbuses to connect loading dock to the ground.

**Step-Back Lintel:** Traces of elegance.

**Stratford Hall:** Westmoreland County, Virginia, 1725. Home of the Lee family and a dream of claiming the land.

**Triangular:** Basic shape of the house fragment.

**T-shirts:** Used as capitals in the new gestural order.

**Under the Portico:** Useful for picnics in the lower meadow; also for porchbuses in bad weather.

**Under the Table:** First dwelling.

**Verisimilitude:** May be lacking.

**Visionary:** Capable of seeing visions; capable of seeing things before they happen; disposed to indulgence in reverie or fancy (Fancy That Reveal); full of imaginative conceptions (could be illusory) as if seen from a *mirador,* up a stair, across a hallway, as a diaphanous gown pacing to the stately rhythms of a cello.

**Wall:** A vertical architectural member used to define and divide space. One of the sides of a room or a building.

**Wing:** A shoulder ornament thought to be an organ of aerial flight. Generally movable, membraneous, paired appendages. One section of a house attached to a central section, possibly a shoulder ornament.

**Wingwall:** Architecture on the move. Coming into the morning on a wing and a quoin.

# The Stratford Fragments: Extravisionary Perception Based on Articulation, Definition, and Wheels

*By Charles Moore and Alice Wingwall*

## The Visionary Made Visible and Buildable

Grand houses, perhaps no longer affordable, should not be destroyed, but should be divided for multiple use. We began by envisioning one wing of a building such as Stratford Hall (Virginia) divided as a duplex, with one unit the mirror image of the other. We then designed a smaller house, artfully arranged, with some movable components which allow a grand sense of domain by their changing positions.

We envision a renewal of figurative sculpture in architecture. We imagine heroic figures portrayed as modular fragments on an annunciatory portal before a house/porch/porchbus complex. The top and central opening of the portal holds a tripartite figure group seen against figurative capitals indicated by torsolike T-shirts.

Cars have become our moving places, very small rooms on wheels, or projectile porches. Indeed, their sense of tight enclosure (protection, memory of house) coupled with movement (speed, toward, into, future, progress) allows a real playing out of dwelling and place fantasies. These wheeled rooms move us across space and across our memories. They move from one building to another and physically attach themselves to new places. They move us and our perceptions of shelter assertively forward, investigating new territory simultaneously with the act of sheltering.

Our car is a porchbus, containing platforms and stairs. When "at home," it allows several directions and combinations of these stairs and platforms. These porchbuses can attach to any other side of the house or porticoes, affording movable places to change with weather conditions, sun patterns, and personal architectural whims. *Alice Wingwall*

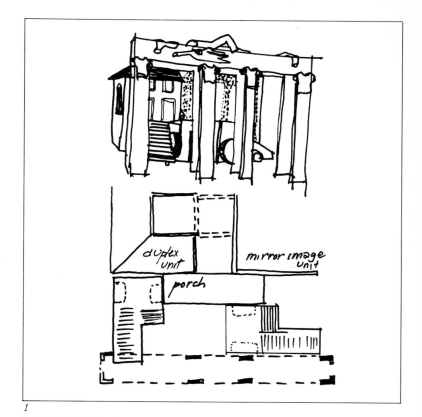

1

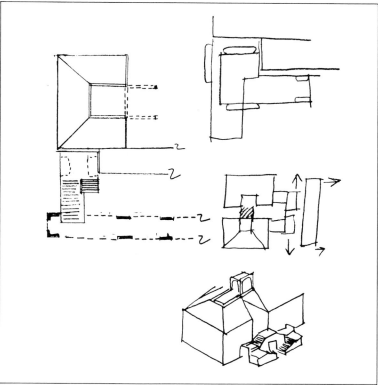

2

*Model and structure fabricators: Mike Bernard, Robin Levitt, Jim Winkler. Photo mural fabricator: Art Lichty.*

1  *Elevation and plan for first scheme for duplex unit, porchbuses, and portico.*

2  *Plans for first scheme of duplex unit based on stairway of Stratford Hall.*

3

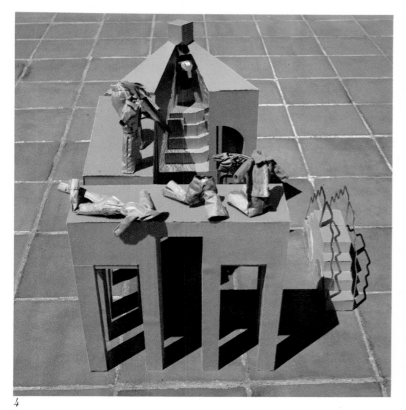

4

5

6

3 Porticoes enclosing an intimate garden space with views framed by allées of portico openings.

4 Porticoes and porchbuses positioned to enclose garden around mirrored stair.

5 House with mirrored stair and movable porticoes and porchbuses for open-cornered garden.

6 A billboard of Palladian dreams corners a garden.

7

7   Perspective elevation of first
scheme of portico/portal with T-
shirt capitals and figured lintel.

8   Elevation of duplex unit
(left) with mirror image unit
(right) and porchbuses as if
seen from portico/portal.

9   Perspective elevation for
first version of duplex unit with
portico and porchbuses.

8

9

There are no stale subjects, only stale artists.... Our collaboration attempts a rich and meaningful allegory for the current condition in the arts. This condition, frequently labeled as Post-Modernist, seeks to recuperate traditional form in order to go beyond the impasse of late Modernization with its belligerently antisymbolic stance, extreme abstraction, and reductionism.

The female figure is cast in bronze; the naturalism of its modeling a clear representation of our continued confidence in the expressive capacity of the Western humanist tradition. The figure surmounts an Ionic column raised on a plinth, both executed in faux marble. Further investigation reveals that the column and base are only partially modeled and appear to be emerging from an asymmetrically composed, scaleless mass sheathed in mirror glass in emulation of the current stage in the evolution of the highrise office block. The contrast between the two systems of composition in the base—the Classicist and the Modernist—is an explicit representation of the disjunction that currently characterizes the arts in general and architecture in particular.

The triumph of mechanomorphology over humanism, so long and so impatiently awaited by the purveyors of the Modern Movement, has not come to pass, while its artistic impact as something "new," free of history and of style, has diminished with the years. The art historical clock cannot be turned back. The "new" has become old, or at least traditional, and Pre-Modernist modes of perception have not disappeared (but merely been eclipsed). Modernism and Classicism now coexist in an uneasy proximity, no longer colliding as opposites but struggling towards a new synthesis.

# Human Scale at the End of the Age of Modernism

*By Robert A. M. Stern and Robert Graham*

1

1  *Side elevation with plans.*

2  *Oblique elevation with figure silhouettes.*

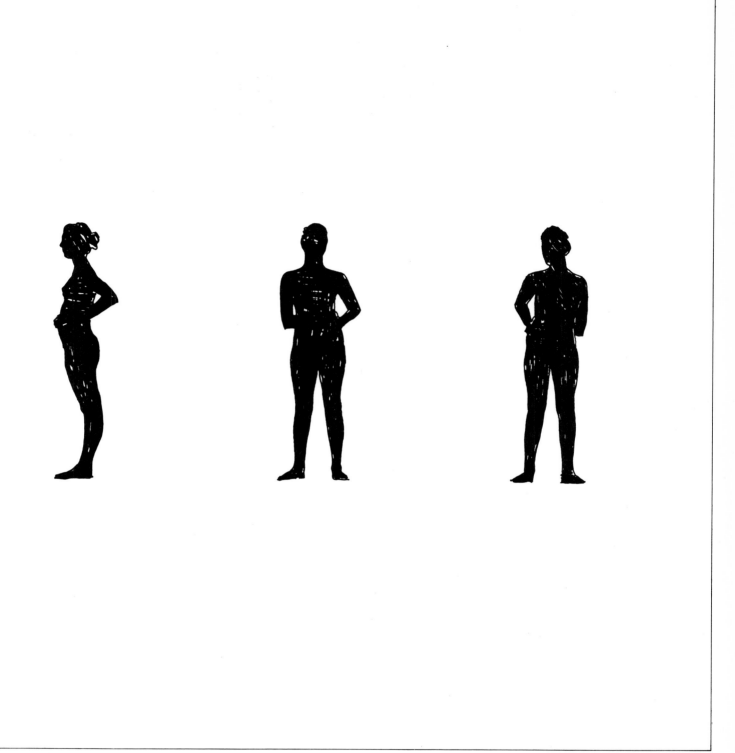

4

3  Model.

4  Silhouette sketches.

It was the intention of William Bailey and Cesar Pelli to produce a work of art not merely sympathetic to the paintings of Bailey, or the architecture of Pelli, but to create a work of art which is a synthesis of each. The formal and aesthetic qualities of the architecture and the paintings should be mutually reinforcing, each responsive to the other in precise ways.

Unlike the traditional relationship between artist and architect (where one or the other art form dominates), Bailey and Pelli pursued their work simultaneously. Each sought to integrate his own artistic intentions with those of the other, to achieve a state where painting informs architecture and architecture informs painting.

The product of this collaboration is a simple hexagonal room of modest size and proportion. Three paintings and three architectural elements (a door and two windows) exist within this space. Each of the paintings and architectural elements is located within alternating walls. Thus a painting is always opposite a window or a door. The paintings and the windows possess an equivalent relationship of size and proportion.

The building is an object on a stone base. The visitor steps up to enter the space. The steeply pitched slate roof is set back from the outer edge of the wall, allowing the mass of the wall to dominate the composition. A flush glass oculus crowns the roof. The wall of horizontal shiplapped siding is taut. Windows and doors are set flush, maintaining the surface of the wall. The interior is of a painted plaster sympathetic to the amber hues of Bailey's paintings. A painted plaster border of a slightly darker hue delimits each segment of the wall.

The composition of each painting is related to its disposition within the room. Opposite the entrance is a single painting of a woman in repose. Her gaze is directed toward the entrance. The painting exists in contraposition to the figure of the visitor framed within the doorway. Flanking the entrance are two still life paintings. Each painting is composed of simple cups and pitchers placed upon a wooden table. The frontality of Bailey's paintings makes these familiar objects architectural. One understands the parallel relationship between the objects upon the table as defined by the painting and works of architecture occupying the landscape as observed through the window.

Many similarities exist between the objects Bailey paints and the room which contains them. Like the room itself, the familiar cups, bowls, and saucers within Bailey's paintings are imbued with a monumental quality. Both the architecture and the painting are direct, rational, and classic.

The light within each painting coincides with the light entering the room. The two still life paintings on either side of the entrance possess an interior light which agrees with that emanating from the closest window. The oculus illuminates the room with soft, diffuse light from above. The painting of the woman is illuminated by a light from above, agreeing with that from the oculus. The paintings echo one another in tonality and proportion, while complementing one another in light and color.

The silence which infuses Bailey's work is an important quality of the room which contains it. Double walls and triple glazing shelter the visitor. The thick, protective walls and simple, static form ensure silence. The room becomes a sanctuary.

The architecture defines the relationship of the visitor to each painting. A table and three chairs stand in the center of the room. Opposite each painting one finds a table, a chair, and a window. Like the frontality of Bailey's paintings the architecture asks the observer to assume a static axial position to each work. Whether the participant is outside the room gazing in, or seated within the space, one relates frontally to the works of art.

The room is a sanctuary, a self-contained object. Though enriched by its context, it is an independent element, able to exist in a variety of settings. Some possibilities are proposed. The room may occupy an urban space or perhaps a traditional courtyard. It may act as an object within the landscape. Or the room may be linked to an existing structure.

William Bailey and Cesar Pelli have created a room, a sanctuary, a place for a dialogue between painting and architecture to occur. It is a place where each discipline may seek in its own way those qualities of clarity, silence, and a slow unfolding. They aspired to unite painting and architecture, to produce a single work of art clear in its intentions and direct in resolution.

# The Hexagonal Room: A Door, Two Windows, and Three Paintings

*By Cesar Pelli and William Bailey*

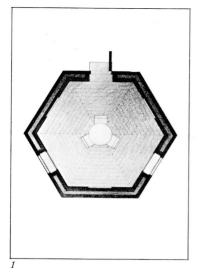

1

2

3

4

1  Plan.

2  Elevation.

3  Section.

4  Still life with hexagonal
room.

5

6

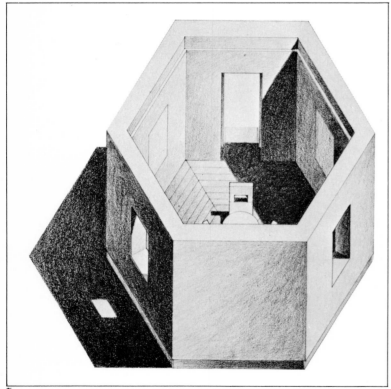

7

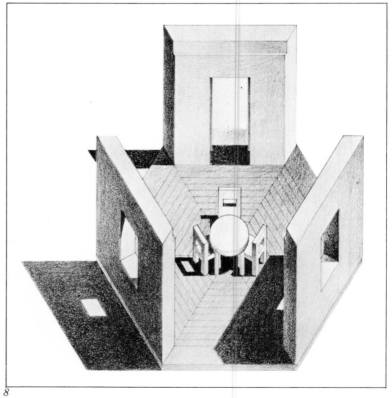

8

**A Room**
*Simple hexagonal room
Interior diameter (across the
flats): 14' 3"
Exterior diameter (across the
flats): 17' 3"
Building height: 18' 10"
Roof: slate shingles on a
pitched roof with glass oculus
Enclosing wall: 1' 6" thick
Exterior wall: painted 4"
shiplapped siding on wood
frame construction
Interior wall: painted plaster
and lath on wood frame
construction
Ceiling: painted plaster
Floors: hardwood
Furnishings: one table with
three chairs*

*Wall hangings: two still life
paintings opposite two windows
and one figure painting
opposite a door*

9

*5–9  Sequential axonometric
drawings.*

*10*

11

10   *Still life through a window.*

11   *A painting and a window.*

12

13

14

12–15  *Examples of potential sites.*

15

For their artist-architect collaboration project, Princeton architect Michael Graves worked with Lennart Anderson, a New York painter. Using the theme of the bacchanal, elements of which appear in previous work by both of them, they juxtaposed the painting and architecture and made them continuous through elaboration of the mutual theme.

I first became acquainted with Lennart Anderson and his work when we were both living and working at the American Academy in Rome in the early 1960s. I have always assumed that our interest in and knowledge of each other's work was of greater benefit to me than to Lennart. I say this because I felt that it was he who contributed most to my understanding of painting in general. I think I was a good student. Even though, at times, our conversations were of an equitable sort, I nevertheless felt that I was primarily the student. It was Lennart who led me through the work of Morandi, Balthus, di Chirico, early de Kooning, and before that, Piero, Mantegna, and Poussin.

In recent years, when discouraged about my alienation from some modern art, I have been able to look at the work of people like Lennart Anderson and feel that I was not alone in my dissatisfaction. In a curious way, we work in a similar manner, in that our compositions do not come easily. We are not facile. And therefore the time spent on any one thing perhaps appears to some as inordinately disproportionate to the object created. However, I suspect that the primary regard that we have for each other's work comes from a sharing of figurative themes that constitute the compositional text of our separate but similar interests. In both our work, there is also a continual examination of the roles of the interior and exterior landscapes. Common to both of us is an interest in the reversal of these roles, in the expansive thematic possibilities of reading or understanding one or the other.

For this particular collaboration, I was aware that Lennart had, for some time, been working on a series of bacchanals. I, on the other hand, had registered in my own compositions those thematic events that are architecturally significant to some of the themes surrounding the bacchanal. In this collaboration, the architect could describe his role in the traditional manner as providing the walls, the rooms, the space within which the painting necessarily takes on additional (that is not to say greater, but only additional) significance than it would have standing alone. Conversely, of course, the architectural setting or composition takes on greater elaboration because of the painter's surface.

The bacchanal was the original feast of the harvesting of the grapes, or more likely of the tasting of the first wine of the season. From the series of specified daily rituals surrounding this event, which developed over time, we find that common objects which we use daily (pitchers, pots, food, tables, etc.) take on amplified importance. It is also thought by some that the idea of drama or theater itself originated in the setting of the bacchanal. The symbolic content of Lennart Anderson's painting and my own architectural composition supporting the theme of the bacchanal has been derived from a chronologic development of the theme. While one senses a somewhat timeless attitude in the painting, one nevertheless senses the ambience of modern time. In the architectural frame for that painting, there is an attitude of being equally timeless and also sustaining an ambience of the archetypal beginnings of the bacchanalian theme. *Michael Graves*

# Bacchanal

*By Michael Graves and Lennart Anderson*

1

1   Bacchanal wall (Lennart
Anderson) with columnar
frame and foreground elements
(Michael Graves).

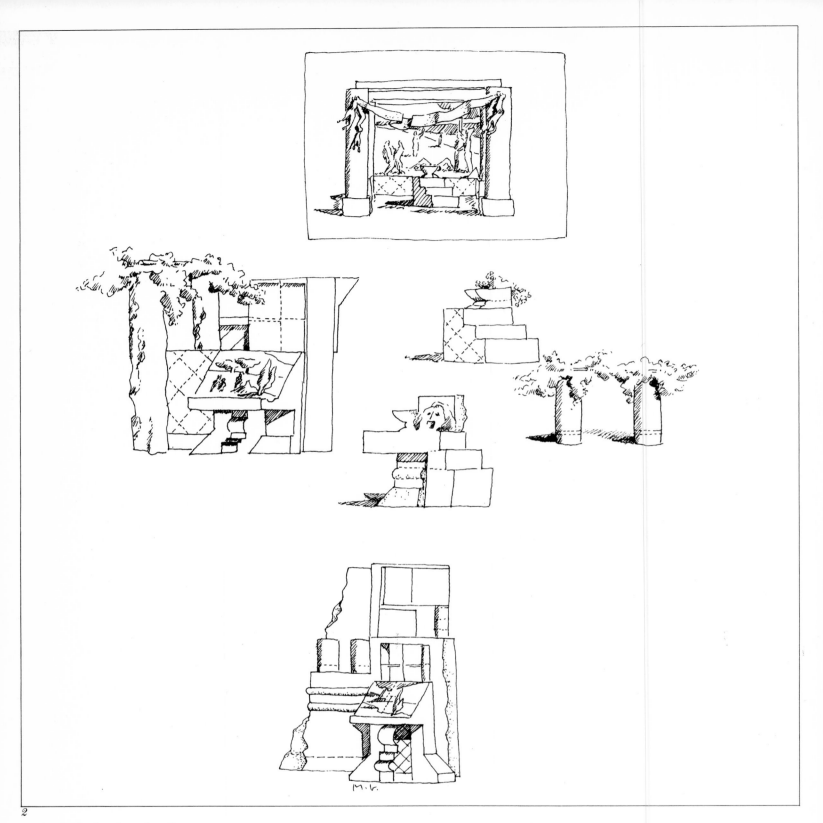

2

2   Study for bacchanal wall
(top); studies for bacchanal
easel (middle left and bottom);
studies for thematic elements
(middle right).

3   Preliminary study.

4   Study of thematic elements
for bacchanal setting.

5   Preliminary study.

3

4

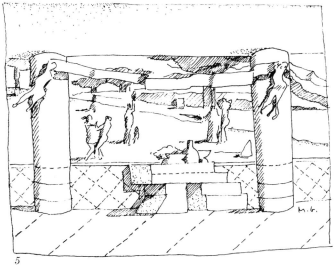

5

## The Tale

The brochure said, "Discover the beauty and enjoy the hospitality of Columbus, the architectural showplace of America. Over forty public and private buildings, each reflecting the creativity and ingenuity of the individual architect, provide the most concentrated collection of contemporary architecture in the world." Asking friends, I learned that all this had come about by the enlightened patronage of J. Irwin Miller, for many years the chairman of Cumming Engine Co., the largest industry in Columbus, Indiana. Taking advantage of an opportunity to lecture in Chicago, I decided to visit Columbus, approximately 250 miles away. I landed in Indianapolis, rented a car, and headed toward the nearby town. As I was driving, images of great cities I have known came to me: Lucca, with its walls and ramparts turned into a delightful elevated ring road; Mantova, almost surrounded by water; Verona, adorned by the remnants of its grand entrance doors; Bologna, the city of porticoes; Ferrara, with the long alley of trees, planted four centuries ago to shade the seasonal movements of its court toward the summer villas. The images were pleasant and the trip therefore short. A sign read "Columbus—6 miles." Getting closer to the city on Route 65 and then 46, I noticed on both sides of the highway two single rows of trees that seemed to have originated deep in the countryside. Slowly they became closer and closer to the road until they began to flank it. The trees were robust and so close to each other that there was a continuous, elevated wall of leaves. Another row separated the highway's two lanes, its foliage extending so high to left and right there was a gauzy canopy over the cars. At a certain moment the road became wider, with four lanes divided by extra rows of trees, so we drove under four canopies side by side. The trees murmured in the wind and filtered sunlight on the passage. I reduced my speed, opened the windows, and let in the air. The trunks marked a ceremonial rhythm. The countryside, thus framed, acquired heightened color values. And the city, announced from afar by four green portals, had that strong meaning only memory can bequeath and the deeper reality only metaphysical gestures can evoke. The

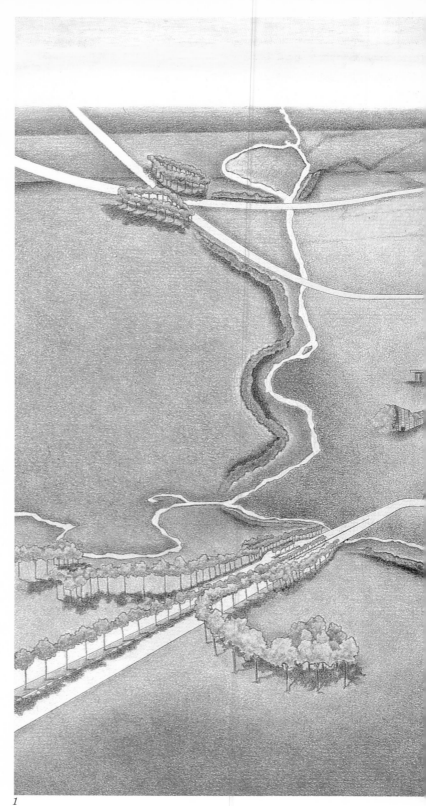

1

# The Four Gates to Columbus

*By Emilio Ambasz and Michael Meritet*

130

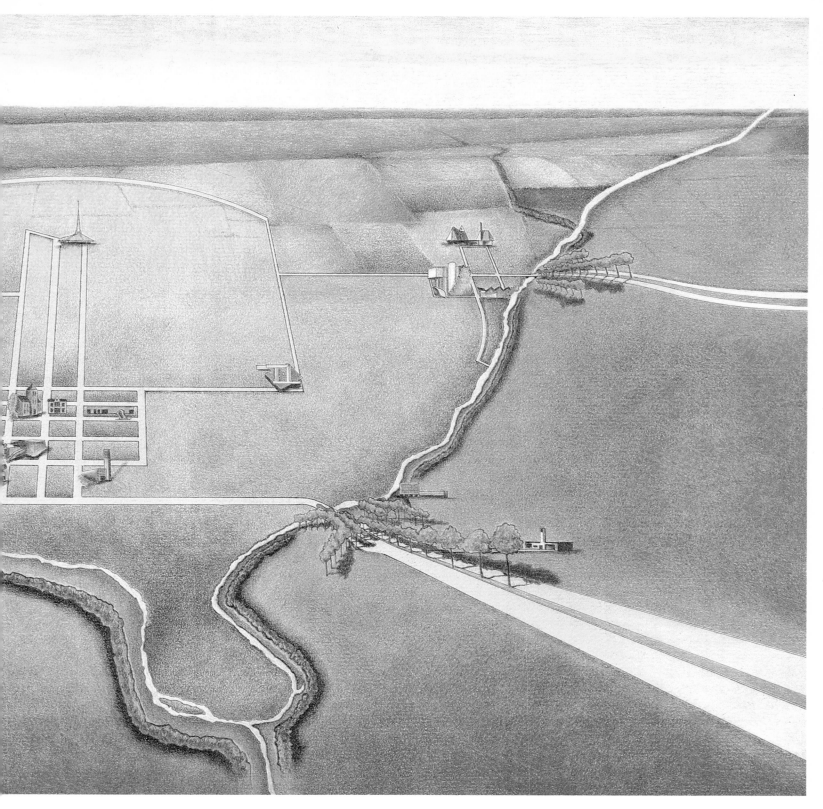

*1   The tale.*

## The Myth

The Gate to the East: through this gate we all came in.

The Gate to the West: through this many of our children left.

The Gate to the South: through which the sun comes.

The Gate to the North: through which we shall all leave someday.

entrance ritual was completed. I had entered.

After passing the city's doors, I observed that the rows of trees bifurcated into a tree-lined belt surrounding the city. Columbus's walls, like its entrance portals, were of living matter. Perhaps more a fence than a barrier. A gentle gesture rather than strong action. A city perimeter delineated by plows rather than blades. The health of the place was visible in its humble love of nature.

Arriving downtown, I entered a covered mall (The Commons). Inquiring, I learned that the city had four such leafy doors, each one different from the next. It seemed to have started some twenty years ago on the basis of a proposal ventured by a New York architect. The townspeople were at first reluctant to define the city's boundaries because they hoped for eternal urban growth. But slowly it became evident to all that the city would derive more strength from knowing its true limits than from an unfocused sense of freedom diluting its center. Once the town agreed on the need to define the city edges and mark its entrances, there were countless discussions. One faction wished to define the city edges by means of a proudly erected construct, circling the city in a manner emblematic of its level of architectural consciousness. Another faction proposed a ring road, with overpasses, bridges, and toll entrances. A third group sustained the notion that no construction of any sort was necessary. They believed it sufficient to evidence the city limits by means of well-designed maps and street signs posted at city edges. Discussions grew in tone and temper until, the story goes, they were all humbled. How this came about is not clear. Some say it happened because the city was the victim of a catastrophic flood. Others claim the town lost its economic base. Still a few believe it happened because the quarrels drove the children to indifference. Be it as it may, the fact is that all groups met and agreed, however uncomfortable at first, to return to the original proposal. By that time the architect who had made the proposal was nowhere to be found. But his designs were left behind.

The scheme was thoughtfully revised so that it might meet with the city's new circumstances, and the resulting plan was approved by all. Everyone was asked to donate at least one tree. School children destined their savings to planting in their parents' name, while parents donated trees in the memory of those deceased. Groups of citizens donated trees to honor beautiful houses which stood no longer while private individuals planted trees to remember caresses received, first loves, forgotten tastes of favorite desserts, generous deeds performed, and vengeful actions repressed.

When first planted, the trees were saplings. When I found them, they were quite grown. In some cases their seeds had already given rise to new saplings. It seems that the townspeople are at present discussing whether to leave the saplings in place so that the emerging forest may slowly reclaim the city or to transplant them to other cities as tokens of Columbus's hard-earned gift for reconciling nature to the human environment.

## History of the Collaboration (or Methodology)

Emilio constructed the *myth*, wrote the *tale*, and illustrated it by means of sketches he called *designs*. Michael then conceived the *images* which give body and depth to the project. (You may say that one wrote the lyrics and whistled the tune, while the other wrote the music and gave resonance to the text.) The "Four Gates to Columbus" exist, so far, in the images and story here represented, the brainchild of a *co-labor*ation. There is nothing that impedes these images from being used as blueprints. Had there been true gardeners at hand, they would have been the recipients of the myth, the tale, and the designs, and the garden they would have been inspired to plant would have been the image. Only through the image can access be gained to the deeper meanings of the myth, the tale, and the design. One cannot have body without the other. The Icon contains all that can be known about the Idea.

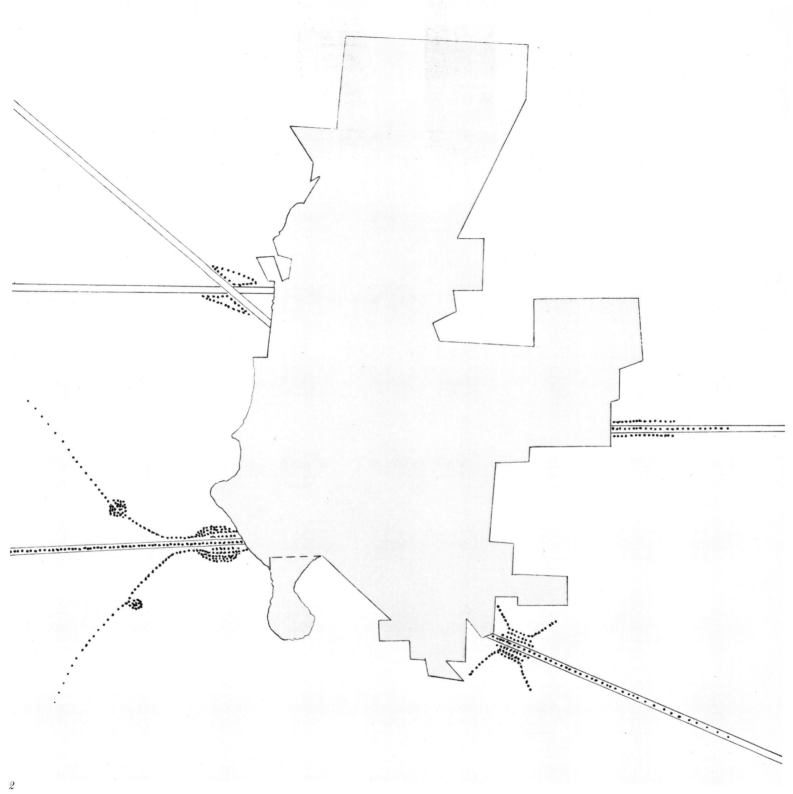

2

2   *The design.*

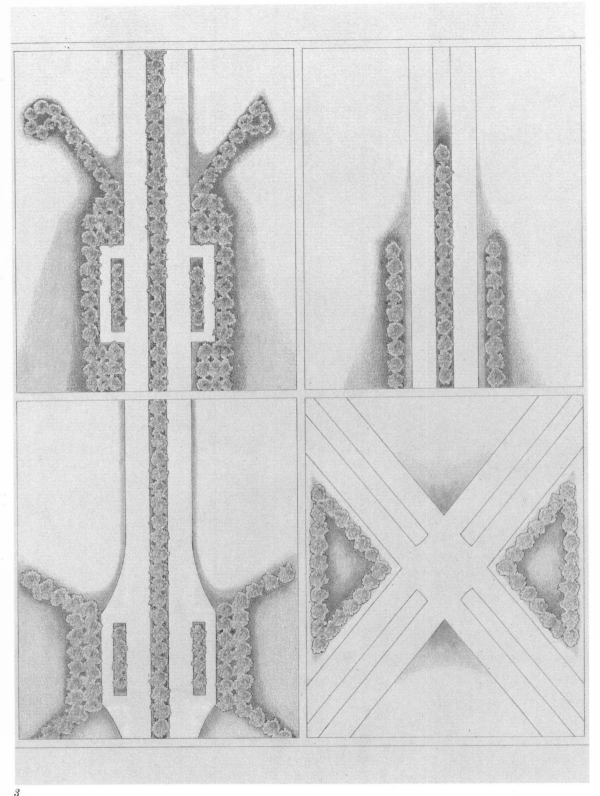

3    *The myth.*

4    *The Gate to the South.*

As in much of the rest of American life, there seems to have been, at least up until now, a certain schizophrenic attitude about the American cemetery. We wish to update the American attitude about death, and for that matter life, since we feel there is no longer any need for the American cemetery to reminisce about earlier cultures. We now sense an America that fell from grace and only then came of age, a maturation of ideals, both formal and ideological.

Just as America and Americans have for so long imported hi-art and good taste from Europe so as to gain legitimacy from its father, thus the American cemetery as well has been the residual of the European sarcophagi, aedicula, and other remembrances of past cultures (Egyptian, Greek, Roman, Romanesque, Renaissance). The art and architecture of a given epoch have always tended to mirror that epoch. In first-century Rome, for example, the buildings for the living as well as the permanent resting places for the dead were based upon the iconography, the decoration and the construction of the time.

Now while America was in the process of coming of age there was every reason to import aedicula art from the very place that the recent emigrants had come. Thus, late-nineteenth-century American art and architecture for the living were a necessary continuance of continental Europe. Artistic and ornamental models were combined with evolving American structural and constructional techniques as a comprehensive representation of the times.

None of this, however, was true of the American cemetery, where objects resembling the Nike Apteros, the cathedral at Rouen, and the Maison Carrée were thought to be sufficiently old to adequately represent a peaceful place of rest for those who had passed from life.

Now, while it is true that avant-garde forms have never been thought of as appropriate as an aedicular for the dead, the case for communicating motifs of traditional quietude can be other than the reshaping of forms representing another time. Obviously, avant garde, modern, or even contemporary formal reproductions as a protective place suggesting perpetuity have not had sufficient time to gain enough legitimacy to represent timelessness.

However, America has developed an entire range of forms within its existing residential typology that we find every bit as appropriate and as dignified for funerary monuments as the traditional Greek, Roman, etc., etc., forms.

Our project for The Architectural League evolved as a product of a series of meetings both in New York at Richard Haas's studio and at my office in Chicago. In our evolving discussion it soon became clear that the project might also become a truly "American" subject, since both Haas and I had, in our own separate ways, appeared to be developing intrinsically American, free-style careers.

Unfortunately, the difficulties of Richard Haas being in New York and me being in Chicago had a certain impact on the concept of "collaboration" such that a meeting finally occurred in my office where he presented an independent proposal for an urban cemetery that he evolved on his own, electing for a "subcollaboration" with New York architect Edward Mills.

However, at that same meeting I proposed drawings based upon extensions of earlier discussions with Haas concerning a suburban typology. It seemed to me to be far more fitting as an "American statement" dealing with life in the city and death on the prairie, dust unto dust, the return to the soil.

The residential typology has been evolving for the entire two centuries of America's existence, and while it began as a necessary extension of the Europe the early American had departed from, it ultimately evolved into a set of forms which became wholly American, such that its duplication into subtypes has reversed the trend of America's hi-culture importation. Levittown now exists not only in New Jersey but in Belgium and France as well.

Thus, through repetitive usage, this funerary typology has, we feel, gained a recognizable credibility such that its transfer into "the little house" as funerary monument is appropriate.

Europe is dense and thus is represented by architecture and urban studies of like architectural appropriateness attacking the problems of density. America is sparse and the purpose of our project here is as a suggestion of the microscopic European emigrant fleeing the density of that continent for

# The Great American Cemetery

*By Stanley Tigerman and Richard Haas*

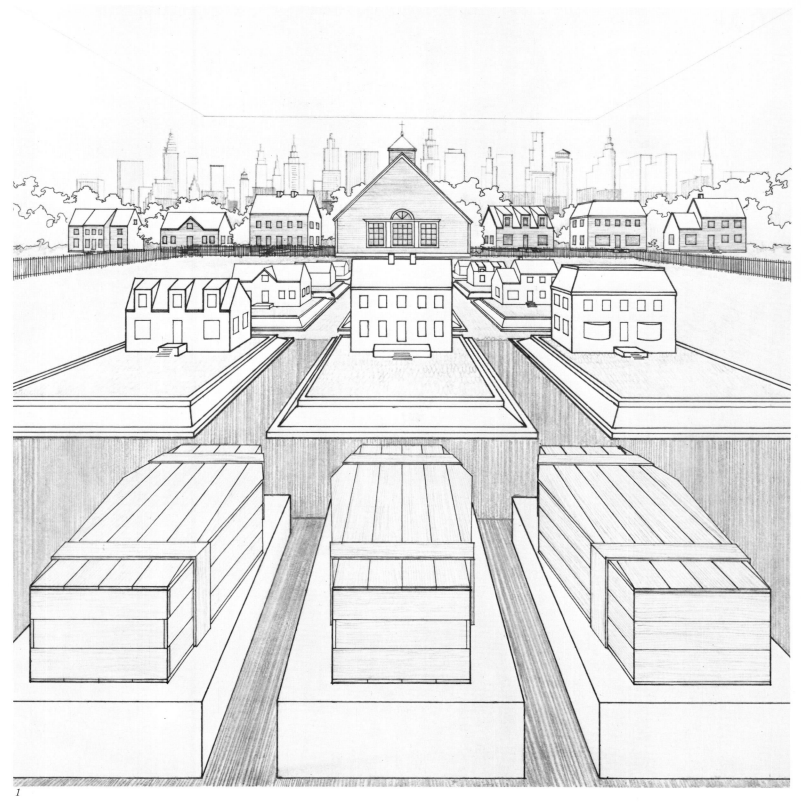

1

1   A typical study of an American cemetery.

the sparsity of this one. The project can also be thought of as the single emigrant fleeing from the collective morality supported by attitudes of "the good of the many" as that emigrant flees toward the strength of the individual, that is, "the good of every single one of us." Therefore, our project may further be seen as the fleeing from the city toward the suburb as one moves through life back toward the soil from which we all sprang. For us the city is life and the land perpetual peace.

Coming out of that meeting we both agreed that Haas's earlier independent collaboration with Mills would be used as explicating both the nature and the difficulties of long-distance collaboration, but that we would now focus upon the suburban concept for further development in dealing with an "America-Come-Of-Age." *Stanley Tigerman*

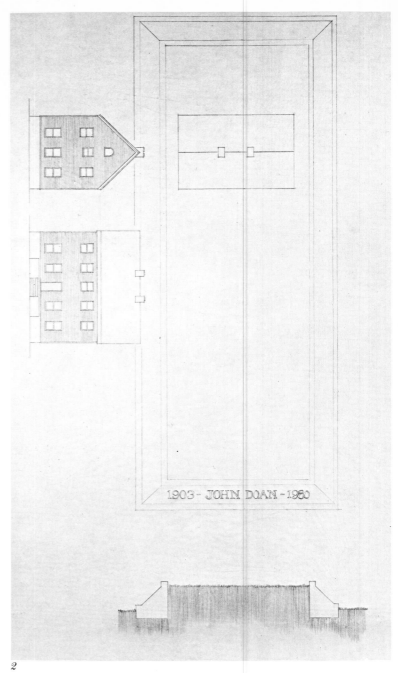

2

2   *Plan and elevation of a typical cemetery plot.*

## An Urban Cemetery: Background to Project

The collaboration between Stanley Tigerman and myself began with two meetings in which we planned to discuss our respective ideas and different areas of focus for the project. During our first meeting, we discovered a mutual fascination with the subject of the American cemetery and its relevance as a theme for American architecture. At our second meeting, little progress was made toward a unified concept or agreement as to the division of our talents on the project. Over the next two months, conflicting schedules kept us from proceeding further, and it soon became clear that Tigerman's view of the cemetery was in a suburban context while I emphasized the need for an urban cemetery. As the deadline approached, Stanley suggested we pursue our divergent concepts of the American cemetery individually. From that point on, I focused on the urban cemetery and assumed he would concentrate on the suburban.

The struggle between being in the center and at the same time wanting to escape from it represents to some degree the conflict of most urban Americans. Among other manifestations, this pervasive conflict is reflected in the design of our cemeteries. It is the struggle which directly influenced the creation of vital urban centers, the growth of suburbia and exurbia, and the retreat to the idyllic wilderness areas of our country.

Since I am not an architect, urban planner, or designer, I made the decision to consult an architect and collaborator: Edward Mills of Voorsanger & Mills, Architects, in New York was my choice. Extensive discussion surrounding the urban cemetery—its philosophical and sociological roots and implications, prospective sites, etc.— immediately followed our decision to collaborate. Our aim is to bring the cemetery closer to the urban core and reflect a condensed version, a microcosm of the city and its structure while offering urban visitors a sense of quiet and repose.
*History and Future Trends:* The movement from the churchyard cemetery to the early nineteenth-century picturesque, romantic cemetery on high ground overlooking the city was the last major innovation of Anglo-American cemeteries. These cemeteries (such as Greenwood in Brooklyn, Mt.

Auburn in Boston, Metarie in New Orleans) exuded a popular parklike atmosphere that attracted people for weekend picnics as well as for grave visitations. This use of the cemetery as a social environment predated the great city in most cases and suburban parks as well. In many ways, the garden cemetery became a nineteenth-century suburbia for the dead.

With predictions that in twenty-five years there will be several cities in the world populated by 20 to 30 million people and more than a dozen cities of 10 million or more inhabitants, the need to focus on a cemetery for the large urban center seems obvious. The cemetery must be brought closer to the greatest number of people and should be concentrated but at the same time remain a peaceful place to visit. *Richard Haas*

## Description of the Project

The cemetery has throughout history mirrored the architecture of the society that built it. The topography of the cemetery, much like the city, is always in a state of flux. Both the city and the cemetery are complex, ever-evolving organisms which reflect fluctuations in the ideology of building for the living and the dead.

The need for order amid the "houses of the dead" has led to definite forms and massing which is analogous to the 20th Century City. The need for centrality is expressed in the tower forms, the tightness of the site, and the pure, concentrated form of the pyramid. The concept of the modern nucleus of the central city comprising all the necessary functions supportive of modern life is being transposed to the "city" for the dead. The towers rising out of the ground and into the sky are symbolic of the passage of the dead from an earthly world to another realm of being.
*Site:* The site for the cemetery is off the southern tip of Roosevelt Island in the East River, across from the island of Manhattan. The cemetery is linked to Roosevelt Island via a long causeway which allows the cemetery to be approached with a solemn awareness of its monumental nature. The same entrance serves as a receiving area for all visitors to the cemetery, and when the deceased are transported to the site, they are taken below to

be prepared for services and interment.

The actual site is a symbolic representation of the street system implemented in our present-day cities: overlayed radial arms extend from the pyramid to the cardinal points. This guided system is made up of solids and voids; the solids are landfill and the voids, water. At the end of each axis we find major monuments to the five predominant religions: Christianity, Judaism, Islam, Buddhism, and Hinduism. Other major tombs and monuments are located within the grid. At the entrance to the site, just off the causeway, are a pair of obelisks which serve the dual function of symbolically "guarding" the entrance and pointing upward to the sun, stars, and heavens.

*The Sanctuary:* The center volume with its pyramid shape constructed of clear glass conveys an image of a shimmering giant object reflecting the towers of the dead and the sky. The material usually comprising a pyramid shape is opaque; however, by constructing this pyramid from glass, we see the meaning of the form is expanded from that of a "solid," clearly defining the space around it, to that of a form which allows space to be defined from both the inside out and the outside in.

The sanctuary is a multifunctional monument to be used for funeral, civil, and religious ceremonies. Once inside the sanctuary (the glass pyramid) we find a centralized, layered form of topiary crowned with a natural dome of branches that have no leaves. This natural temple serves as a chapel, gravesite, and garden. The center of this forest temple is a dark void, echoing the dark path of the dead.

*The House of the Dead:* Growing out of the glassy volume of the pyramid are twelve towers, each 30° apart and located at the true cardinal points. The number 12 is meant to signify the twelve months and the passage of time as well as the minimum number of points to define a pure circle.

Four of the towers are taller than the others, to symbolize the four seasons (another analogy to the passage of time). These towers are reminiscent of our modern urban apartment towers and office buildings; one is laid to rest here in a form similar to that in which one worked and lived. These towers are constructed of granite and varied tones of marble. Their vertical ascent is much like that of

natural life forms—reaching toward the sun.

Each tower houses repositories for the interred bodies and ashes. The towers are comprised of 30,000 burial vaults, with each tower containing one central elevator stopping at all floors. Each floor has three levels of burial vaults upon which epitaphs are engraved as well as on the walls of the rooms. The towers also contain columbaria on each floor, housing the ashes for another 30,000 people.

There are observatories at the top floors of each of the four tallest towers. These serve as commemorative platforms, allowing the visitors to observe the living city from the sanctuary of the dead. The impact of the transition from the realm of the known to that of the unknown is most strongly felt from these heights.

*The Future of the Past:* It is said that those who do not remember the past are condemned to repeat it. This is one aspect of the past that we are all condemned to repeat, remember, and never lose sight of. It is an existential issue because it touches the core of everyone's existence and reflects a profound commonality and universality. Few aspects of life are more studied, written about, talked about, feared—and few are the subject of greater controversy. Death is the fate of all humankind and we are all joined together by it even in life. Hence the importance of the cemetery and our belief that it should serve the living left behind as well as those who have died.

After completing work on the design of the urban cemetery, there were two subsequent meetings in Chicago with Stanley Tigerman in which we collaborated on the presentation for the suburban cemetery. We agreed that we needed a unified exhibit and decided to focus on the suburban format as a three-dimensional diorama.

Two additions that we agreed upon were made to the miniature cemetery. These were a city skyline as backdrop and a collective crypt beneath the individual grave plots, which were included to indicate a sense of the cemetery being located away from the congested center. Also, each plot would be occupied for a period of time before entering the collective crypt. This scheme was derived from the functioning of churchyard cemeteries of Central Europe, which have been in operation for centuries. *Edward Mills and Richard Haas*

Subproject Team:
Richard Haas
Edward Mills

Bartholomew Voorsanger
John Holland
Medéa Eder

3

3   Axonometric view of cemetery island showing causeways
and reflecting ponds within the
river.

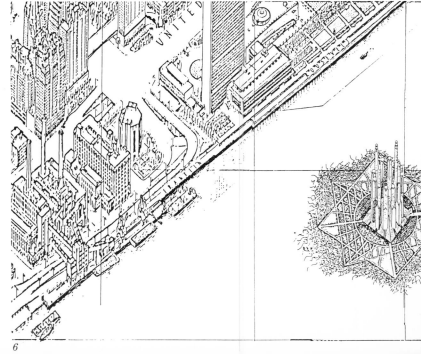

5

4  *View of cemetery at night.*

5  *Interior of pyramid showing topiary garden with dome covered with foliage.*

6  *Site plan for urban cemetery located in East River off 42nd Street and Roosevelt Island.*

RIVER

The project began with a series of discussions between us, creating a dialogue where we often challenged each other's assumptions. Ellis Island was envisioned as a scaffold and as a propitious screen for the projection of themes we had identified in an early proposal. We saw these themes as a common thread in our respective work and as the basis for the project's hypotheses: The City/The Wilderness, The Built/The Natural, Tradition/History, Art: Architecture/Society.

At this time we concerned ourselves not so much with a program for the site but with general questions: for example, what constitutes a monument, what was the image of America for the early wave of immigrants, what was the reality they found, and what is our reality now? Together we evolved through argument and sketches a repertory of images, or rather *emblems*. The positive energy of our exchanges needs to be emphasized. For although it is possible to trace the precise authorship of each image, they would not have occurred in that form outside our discussions.

The island was imagined as a one-story thick platform covered with a gridiron pattern of concrete pavers. On this platform only the Immigration Station would remain, vacant and windswept, populated by sparrows. The building would be intersected with a landscape following the natural outline of the original island. Neither the landscape nor the building would be the dominant figure; they would be meshed in a permanent present.

On the other side of the island the platform's section would form a two-sided amphitheater of high and deep steps, enclosing a long, rectangular green space where events of special relevance to different ethnic groups would be celebrated. On the amphitheater's upper terrace would be telephone booths where visitors, upon dialing a certain number, would receive information on their families' origins.

Underneath this synthetic expression of the collective we imagined a labyrinth of information, a teeming place where historical events and personal recollections would coexist and become interchangeable. At every turn there would be the surprise of a long forgotten event or a constantly remembered one. Information about the remotest past would be located in the labyrinth's central zone, running the length of the island. Entries and exits to either side would be made through areas closest to the present—today's news. Ordinary storefront doors extrapolated from the suburban commercial landscape would lead the unsuspecting visitor from the central green and the island's edges to the internal labyrinthian corridors.

In the area that joins both sides of the island there would be a forest as an emblem of America, the Natural Paradise, while a rainbow would celebrate Ellis as gateway to the New World.

The Ellis Island of the project's early stage was a metaphorical landscape (not unlike Brecht's *Mahagonny*) where the multiple, seemingly uncontrollable, and complex facts of reality were distilled to those images that were seen as essential to the expression of the *idea*. The emblems, taken as a totality, constituted an icon of utmost clarity. Here we arrived at a sensitive point, because the challenge to create a response in terms of architecture raised the question of the icon's plausibility—if not as an idea—as an actual place. In the architect's view, a thoughtful consideration of contextual facts such as the size, proportions, and location of salvageable buildings within the site, the National Parks Service policies about preservation and development of the island, the likelihood of financing by public and private sources, and the reconciliation of diverse interest group requirements would force a transformation of the emblems and the total image they formed.

At this point, a divergence of attitudes about the next stage of development, if any, caused the collaboration to break down. The artist was satisfied with the project and was in favor of preserving the integrity of the idea in its entirety. The architect decided to continue, confronting the idea with the contextual conditions outlined above.

Inevitably, her own understanding of architecture as a public art as well as the meaning of designing a park within the historical continuum begun with the *pleasure garden* and followed by the *reform park*, the *recreational facility*, and the *open space system*[1] influenced the project's form during this stage. The design itself shows to what extent both reality and emblems were transformed as a consequence of their confrontation with each other.

[1]These are categories developed by Galen Cranz in "Changing Roles of Urban Parks: From Pleasure Garden to Open Space," *Landscape* 22, no. 3 (Summer 1978).

# Ellis Island: Gateway to America

*By Susana Torre and Charles Simonds*

## Ellis Island

*Ellis Island was the principal point of entry for immigrants to the United States from 1892 to 1954. Through its gates passed 16 million people—most of them poor, many of them displaced by political and economic events in their homelands—to begin new lives in the New World. Today, the survivors among these immigrants and their descendants comprise nearly half the United States population—an estimated 100 million out of 218.5 million—making Ellis Island one of the most widely shared historical experiences of the American people.*

*Ellis Island sits in New York Harbor, only 1,000 yards away from the Statue of Liberty. Its area, roughly equivalent to five New York City blocks, is divided into two equal parts by a ferry slip. The main Immigration Station in the northwest half was designed by Boring and Tilton, winners of a competition called with the intention of improving the design quality of government buildings. The southwest side of the island contains the main hospital building, where immigrants were detained for medical or political reasons, and the contagious disease wards, formed by several separate pavilions connected by a covered corridor.*

*After its closing in 1954 Ellis Island was declared surplus federal property and offered for public sale. Since then, proposals for Ellis Island's transformation have included, among others, a women's prison, a drug rehabilitation center, a home for the aged, a college, legalized gambling, Frank Lloyd Wright's City of Tomorrow, Philip Johnson's Wall of the 16 Million, and John F. Kennedy's Island of Racial Equality.*

*The island was declared a National Monument in 1965 and placed under the jurisdiction of the National Parks Service of the Department of the Interior, whose policies have oscillated between a 1968 proposal to demolish all buildings except the Immigration Station and to transform the island into a green park and the current policy of conservation and adaptive reuse of existing structures. The future development of Ellis Island is of great importance since, together with the Statue of Liberty, it will become the centerpiece of Liberty State Park's crescent. The park, now being built on the New Jersey shore, is expected to increase the already large number of visitors to the Statue and Ellis Island.*

*Project Assistants: Kevin Gordon, Deborah Dietsch, and Ana Steinschraber.*

*Special thanks are due to Michael Adlerstein of the National Parks Service, Richard Plunz of Columbia University School of Architecture and Planning, Geoffrey Fox, Ray Beeler, Bryan McGrath, and Lorna McNeur.*

*The text for "Ellis Island" and "Brief Chronology" was freely excerpted from the report prepared for the National Parks Service by Harlan Unrah, Richard Plunz's studio brief, a National Parks Service brochure on Ellis Island, and other sources.*

*Photograph taken circa 1904 showing immigrants waiting to enter the main building.*

| | 1812–1890 | 1890–1897 | 1897 |
|---|---|---|---|

  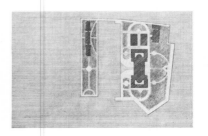

*Construction of Fort Gibson began before the outbreak of war in 1812 to replace an earlier fortification built during the Napoleonic wars as a deterrent to naval attack by Great Britain. During the Civil War Fort Gibson was used as a supply station and naval arsenal. In 1890 Congress voted to remove the arsenal from Ellis Island and relocate the immigration depot from Castle Garden in Battery Park to Ellis. The public's intense fear of an explosion at the fort's powder magazine and its apprehension of the increased influx of destitute immigrants arriving in the city prompted this decision.*

*The island's area is increased to accommodate the first Immigration Station. Opening in 1892, the building was designed by a government architect to handle 10,000 immigrants in a day. This "latter day water place hotel," as it was described at the time, was surrounded by small structures recycled from military uses into hospital, detention, and auxiliary buildings. The island's pointed shape stands as a reminder of the fort's garrison wall. The station was completed June 13, 1897. Two days later the island was swept by fire and virtually all buildings and immigration records were destroyed.*

*The project submitted by the New York firm of Boring and Tilton won the closed competition for the design of the second Immigration Station. The other invited participants were McKim, Mead, & White, Carrère and Hastings, Bruce Price, Alfred Barlow, and John L. Smithmeyer. The program called for two fireproof buildings—the station and a hospital—and service structures. The station posed a problem "quite without precedent," but "the central feature is the same as that of a railroad station: the requirements of landing, collecting and distributing large, sudden crowds," in the architects' words. The removal of all small-scale buildings (with the exception of the power house) because of the fire provides the clean slate for a City Beautiful axial composition. The artificially enlarged island is viewed as a pedestal for a monumental ensemble in the French Renaissance style. The project was regarded as one of the most important represented at The Architectural League's exhibition of 1899.*

*1–2 Maps showing location of Ellis Island in New York Harbor.*

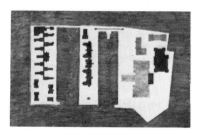

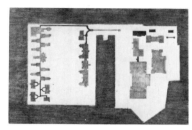

*Construction of the Immigration Station and Hospital was based on a modified site plan. In the view of the contemporary press the main building symbolized "lavish hospitality and world-wide welcome." The building's stone-trimmed arched windows have their precedent on both sides of the Atlantic: Paris's Gare Montparnasse of 1855 and Gare du Nord of 1863, Boston's Union Station, and New York's Penn Station by McKim, Mead, & White. The building's imposing towers recall an earlier use of towers as gateways in nineteenth-century American train stations as well as the building's major influence: the Electricity Building by Van Brunt and Howe at the Chicago World's Columbian Exposition of 1893. The main building opened in 1900, followed by the adjacent Kitchen, Restaurant, Bath, and Laundry Building, and the Power House in 1901 and the Main Hospital in 1902.*

*From the beginning the island became a perennial construction site. Additional structures were added more as a result of improvisation than long-term planning. Work began on a new island in 1905, and a group of detached pavilions used as contagious disease wards was completed in 1909. The design of the main building and hospital was altered with multiple renovations and additions. During the years before World War I immigration rose to more than one million annually, spurred by the country's rapid growth and expansion of labor-intensive industries. During the war there was a sharp decline in immigration, and the island was used to hold in custody the crews of German merchant ships and suspected enemy aliens and as a treatment facility and way station for returning American soldiers.*

*The quota laws of 1921 and 1924 ended mass immigration, changing the principal function of Ellis Island to that of deportation center. The landfill between Islands 2 and 3 was completed at this time. Landscaping and playgrounds were added with Work Progress Administration (WPA) funds and labor, together with building improvements recommended in an evaluation prepared by a committee of prominent citizens selected by Frances Perkins, Secretary of Labor. A mural by Edward Laning depicting* The Role of Immigrant in the Industrial Development of America *was completed in 1938.*

*Construction included a recreation building and shelter on the filled-in area between Islands 2 and 3, a new ferry house at the head of the boat slip, and an immigration building never used for this purpose behind the ferry house. The island's area is further increased and its shape rendered almost perfectly symmetrical. During World War II the facilities were used as a Coast Guard Station, a hospital for returning wounded soldiers, and a detention center for suspected enemy aliens. The covered walkways were built at this time. The Public Health Service closed the main hospital in 1951. The Immigration and Nationalization Act of 1952 and a liberalized detention policy enacted two years later resulted in the official and definitive closing of Ellis Island in 1954.*

1

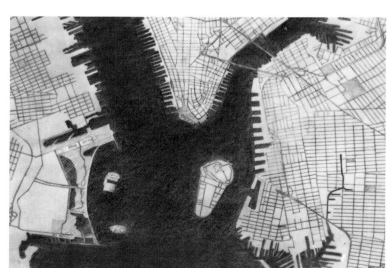

2

## The Architectural Project:
## A Public Park on Ellis Island

The project proposes the transformation of Ellis Island, a place of hope and despair, into a place of remembrance and celebration. If built, this park would be the first to celebrate in its design and proposed uses the plurality of influences that have shaped a civilization.

Half of the island is retained as museum, the main Immigration Station left empty, filled with silence where names of every nationality were once shouted. Upon exiting the building through the low railroad addition, the visitors find themselves at the edge of a reflecting pool that follows the outline of Fort Gibson's wall, built in 1812. Beyond is a high wall with a walkway atop supported by shallow masonry arches on one side. This wall follows the outline of Ellis Island during the building of the Immigration Station and the years of peak immigration influx.

The visitors may walk beyond this wall by following the curved walkways, a fragment of the intended but never built garden. In so doing, they will pass under the flag—a reenactment of the immigrants' rite of passage and their confrontation with the values of a civilization as yet unknown to them. Beyond the wall is a grassy area with a wooden boardwalk intended to recall the loading docks where many immigrants waited to be transported to the mainland. The walkway above the wall, accessible from stairs and ramps, functions as a vantage point to view Manhattan and the Statue of Liberty, restoring to the singular prowlike shape its meaning as carrier of an earlier memory of the site: Fort Gibson's garrison wall and gun battery.

Only those buildings that were part of Boring and Tilton's site plan have been retained on the northwest side of the island and a sense of the original composition preserved through selective restoration. On the southwest side the main hospital building is redefined as a public palace, housing the Administration, The Center for the Study of American Ancestry (where visitors have access to computer terminals to find out about their families' origins), and a Youth Hostel.

The central, green space will be used for picnics, parades, concerts, games, and festivals. This space marks the intersection of the two major influences on American attitudes toward landscape. Along the southwest-northeast axis it is experienced as the ceremonial foreground to a formal garden beyond, while along the northwest-southeast axis it functions like town and college greens, recalling Jefferson's plan for the University of Virginia with a prominent building at its head. Narrow pools beside the long edges of the green suggest the once separate islands.

The garden opposite the former hospital has an oval pool with a 24-foot high waterfall around its edge. The monumental stairs at the center lead to checkered terraces of paving and grass to either side, forming a stadium in which to view the events occurring in the central green, and to an upper terrace, also accessible by a ramp. Here is a labyrinth garden, the archetypal form associated with the act and process of dwelling. It is formed by three patterns. The first consists of paths 10 feet wide flanked by trees, leading from one edge of the garden to its opposite and to centers with small fountains and seating. The second is a hedge labyrinth with paths 4 feet wide and 6 feet high. The third is a small turf maze intended as a children's playground.

Below the labyrinth garden is a building accessible from two entrance pavilions at either end of the terraces. These pavilions enclose entrance courtyards leading to the interior, a flexible space defined by a 24-foot structural module housing temporary and permanent exhibitions, display and seminar rooms of many ethnic, regional, national, and international organizations including the American Museum of Immigration.

The edge of the island facing the Statue of Liberty functions like a ship's deck lined with various small ethnic restaurants and shops. Along this street the visitors may pause and enjoy an imaginary voyage while relaxing and eating on the deck's upper level. The street is only interrupted at its center, behind the great waterfall. Water pumped from the sea to form the waterfall is recycled through large circular openings in the seawall.

Either at their arrival or at their departure from

the island the visitors may stop at the restored Art Deco ferry house to view an audiovisual presentation about Ellis Island's history or buy postcards and souvenirs. They may also enjoy a walk through the forest facing New Jersey, a reminder of the American wilderness cherished by Europeans and Americans alike at the turn of the century. Finally, they may participate in an event taking place at the bermed building that is at the head of the central green. This building is the transformed ruin of the former recreation structure where immigrants enjoyed some sociability and entertainment. The 45° berm covering the building's sides is planted with 3-foot high "Christmas tree" pines. Stairs lead to an upper balcony around the

building's perimeter and mark the entrance. As one enters through an opening in the hearth, the skylight above fills the buried building with light.

On special occasions like the Fourth of July or the anniversary of the Statue of Liberty's dedication, powerful water cannons at either end of the island shoot a spray into the air causing a rainbow to form.
*Susana Torre*

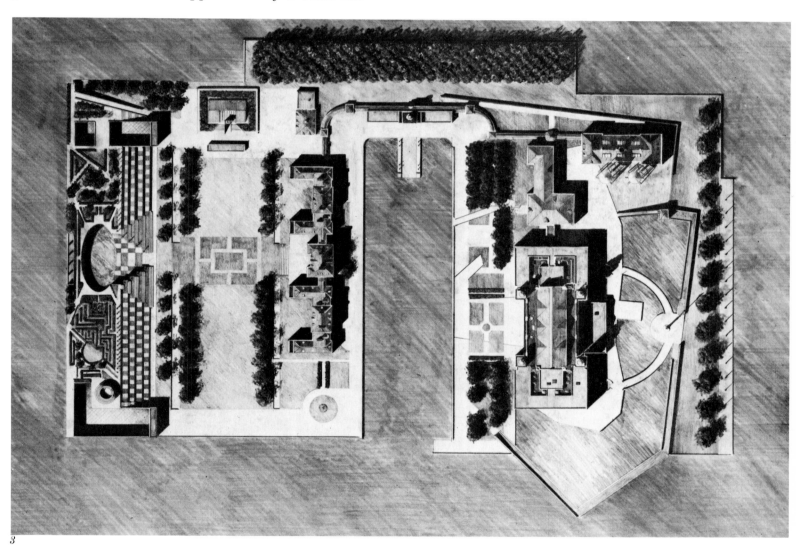

3

*3 Proposal for a public park in Ellis Island: site plan. Key to the plan: (1) Ferry arrival; (2) Restored ferry house; (3) Immigration Station; (4) Outline of Fort Gibson's wall (1812–1890); (5) Outline of Ellis Island (1900–1920); (6) Flag pole; (7) Walkways; (8) Reflecting pool; (9) Outlook; (10) Ramps; (11) Grass and wooden boardwalk; (12) Restored Power House; (13) Restored Kitchen, Restaurant, Bath, and Laundry Building; (14) Services; (15) Entry to garden, Administration above; (16) Center for the Study of American Ancestry; (17) Youth Hostel; (18) Shallow pools; (19)* *Town Green; (20) Oval pool and waterfall; (21) Monumental stairs; (22) Checkered terraces; (23) Labyrinth garden (turf maze is below the oval pool in the drawing); (24) Aviary; (25) Entrance pavilions; (26) Entrance courts; (27) "Ship's deck" street, restaurants, and shops; (28) Restored recreation shelter; (29) Bermed recreation building; (30) Forest; (31) Water cannons; (32) Commemorative statues.*

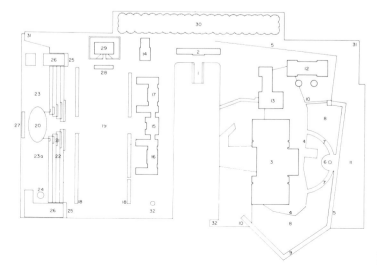

4

5

6

4 Proposal for a public park in
Ellis Island: view toward the
Statue of Liberty.

5 Proposal for a public park in
Ellis Island: view toward
Liberty State Park.

6 Proposal for a public park in
Ellis Island: view toward
Manhattan.

Times Square was chosen as the theater for our operations for its mythic possibilities and its complex content and form. It is both a crossroads of the city and a cross section of our media- and commodity-oriented culture; it occupies a central position in our imagination when we think of the wonders of the urban world. It has evolved from a historic process of abrasions and has become a monument impossible to reconstruct or orchestrate.

One can suppose a world where desire and fantasy are immediately gratified—a paradisical state. Times Square as a broadcaster of cultural desires and fantasies that it does not and, in fact, cannot satisfy is a sham Garden of Eden. Rather than making Times Square acceptable, we have chosen to accept Times Square. We have used the residual spaces and energies that exist in a way that will permit the spectacle and theater of the failed paradise to exhibit itself.

We have chosen the metaphor of a waterworks constructed on the residual traffic islands rising above and falling below the street: made of glass, served by machines, tiered and layered, supported by odd structures, and inhabited by the residents. The islands interrupted by the cross streets, accidentally determined, provide a rigorous system turning accident into ordering device. This device provides connections and disconnections, harmony and dissonance. The waterworks is seen as a meta structure giving back Times Square, simultaneously reflecting it and transparent to it.

The collaborative process was initiated by two preliminary fantasies—speculations on the nature of the Times Square intervention and the echoes of its emanations forward and backward in time. The final collaborative work is a synthesis of the individual fantasies, a process of give and take transmuting the various elements of the private beginnings.

### A Fountain

Once upon a time an Omphalos existed on the island now called Manhattan. The land in those days was both higher and lower. The Omphalos lay in a small valley and was surrounded by a mighty fountain. The fountain was majestic and magisterial—giantlike to our eyes. It fed the Omphalos its funnellike rush of waters. The waters fell and churned over the glassy volutes and arises, the curiously shaped moldings and corners, giving the passing body illusory shape and form. The waters fell uniformly until man found Manhattan.

Over the years inroads were made into the fountain; the land was leveled and alien structures surrounded the Omphalos. Parts of the fountain disappeared, and the remaining parts were propped up and supported by odd methods employed by bemused men who had long ago forgotten what the fragments had been when they were whole.

Finally only slivers of the original were left—archaeologic bits; clumsy machines were rigged to conduct water over these slivers in a sort of perversely memorial gesture. People walked under and over the remnants, lit the supporting trusses, and made use of the gloomy covered spaces. The trusses aged and needed to be braced as the bits of the fountain became more and more fragmented and finally occupied only those spaces that were useless for overt exploitation and were not needed for circulation. They shared their space with other material thrown off by this grouping of peoples.

The Omphalos is now 22 feet below the surface and 6 feet below the invert of a sewer spanning it in an east-west direction. *James Freed*

### The Palace of Versailles Waterworks

Historians long ago began to write the history of the body. They have studied the body in the field of historical demography or pathology; they have considered it as the seat of needs and appetites. . . . But the body is directly involved in a political field; power relations have an immediate hold on it; they invest it, mark it, train it, torture it, force it to carry out tasks, to perform ceremonies, to emit signs. . . . What the apparatuses and institutions operate is . . . a microphysics of power. . . . Now, the study of this microphysics presupposes that the power exercised on the body is conceived not as property, but as strategy, that its effects of domination are attributed not to 'appropriation', but to dispositions, manoeuvres, tactics, techniques, functionings; that one should decipher in it a network of relations, constantly in tension, in activity, rather than a privilege that one might possess; That one should take as its model a perpetual battle rather than a contract regulating a transaction or the conquest of a territory.

Michel Foucault, *Discipline and Punish*

# Two Fantasies of a Mythical Waterworks

*By James Freed and Alice Aycock*

The Palace of Versailles Waterworks is envisioned as an architecture of spectacle and exhibitionism located in Times Square. It is manned by the overflow population from various public institutions. These so-called inmates are vagrants and transients, "down and outers," idle riffraff. They are designated as the operators of the waterworks, which is a vast medieval machine with treadmills and windmills and waterwheels modeled after the Marly Machine built on the Seine River in the seventeenth century.

The inmate operators are assigned numbers and wait in long lines on aisles which run at steep inclines. Someone calls out numbers randomly, and the operator inmates are then assigned performing platforms, stages which are erected at different heights. These staging platforms can be raised or lowered by pulleys. Some have canopies, and during the summer the soft canvas is gathered in billowing folds and strung against the sky like horizontal kites. Actors from the theater district move through the crowd performing fragments of plays.

The inmate operators are given the task of inventing ways to use the water. Their countless inventions and reinventions are based on trial and error. Idle, vacant minds participate in senseless unnecessary labor with arcane mechanical devices. Often there is no connection between the task at hand and the methods employed.

All the actions in the waterworks, both human and mechanical, are repetitive, up and down, back and forth, left and right. Despite the highly patterned, predictable quality of these movements, there are no connections between the various parts of the machine. There are pools of water whose surfaces are marred by false waves. There are large fish in the water, also flying fish, and boats that look like fish. There are rows of hanging boats and acrobats hanging from hoists. The sides of the stepped platforms and sluice gates are covered with cargo nets that inmates clamor down. Some of the platforms have trap doors which release willing participants into the water below. In some places water is raised through a series of large inclined Archimedean screws placed on the stepped platforms. Oversized cups turn over, emptying out and filling up, dumping their occupants into the water and picking them up again. *Alice Aycock*

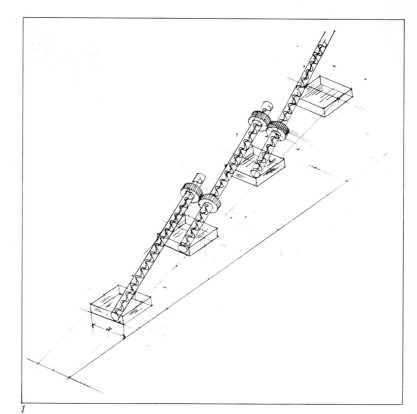

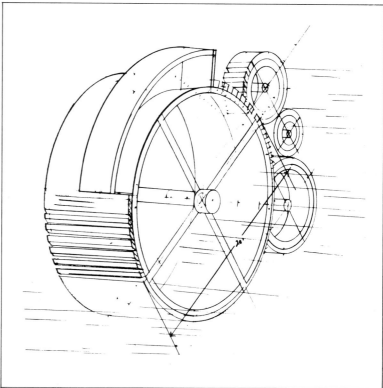

1 Sketch for possible method of raising up water through a system of transparent Archemedeon screws.

2 Sketch for a system of revolving gears with bodyslots located in the sewage treatment pool.

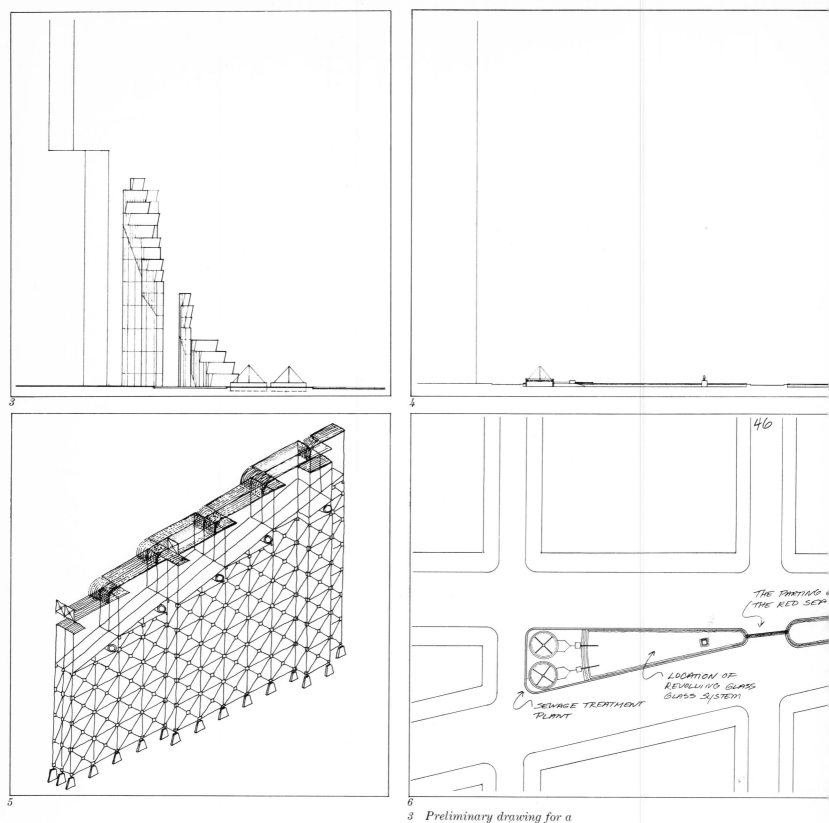

46

THE PARTING
THE RED SEA

LOCATION OF
REVOLVING GLASS
GLASS SYSTEM

SEWAGE TREATMENT
PLANT

3  Preliminary drawing for a
waterworks project for Times
Square: front elevation.

4  Preliminary drawing for a
waterworks project for Times
Square: elevation.

5  Preliminary drawing of iso-
metric detail of possible structure.

6  Preliminary drawing for a
waterworks project for Times
Square: plan.

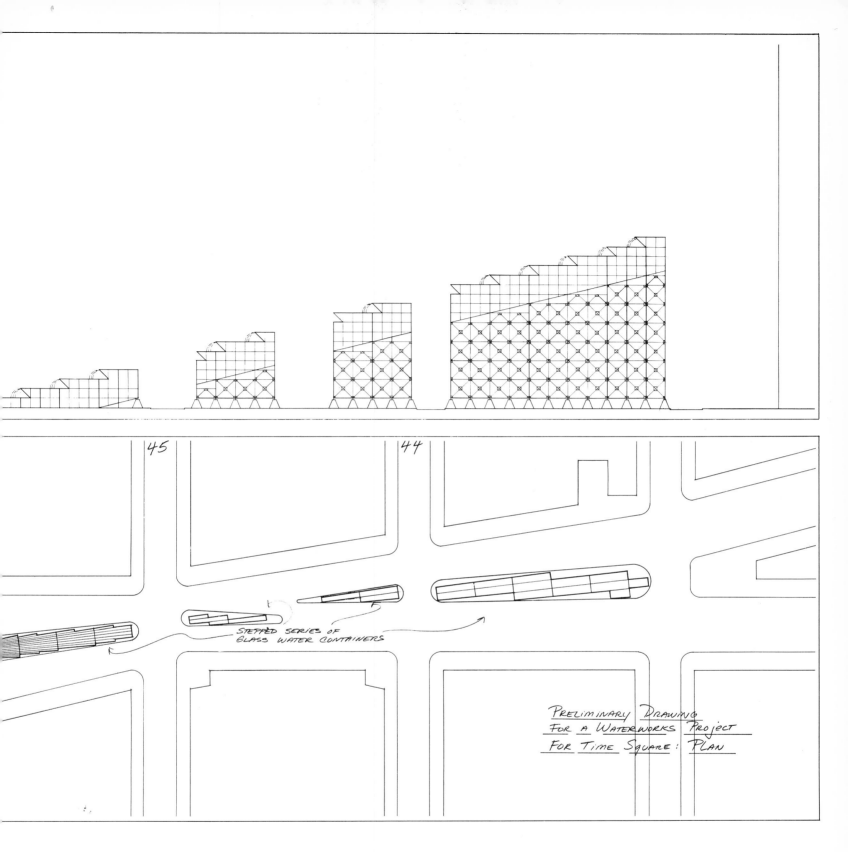

STEPPED SERIES OF
GLASS WATER CONTAINERS

PRELIMINARY DRAWING
FOR A WATERWORKS PROJECT
FOR TIME SQUARE: PLAN

Richard Serra and I have known each other for several years. I am a great admirer of his work and have learned much from him. He, in turn, has seemed curious about my work and occasionally appears to be making gestures of approval as he wanders through my spaces. I was impressed with his interest in architecture and his intense commitment to ferreting out architectural information. In all probability, he is one of the best architecturally informed artists in the country.

A couple of years ago I attended a dinner with Michael Pittas of the National Endowment for the Arts. In the course of our conversation, Michael suggested that I apply for a personal grant. I laughed at him and said, "I could never fill out all those papers; and if I ever did, you would probably not want to fund the project I was interested in."

"Try me," he said. Since Richard Serra was on my mind, I said, "I would like to do a project with Richard Serra." Michael Pittas said, "Fantastic. We'll fund it."

I proceeded to forget about that evening. A year later I was in New York discussing lots of things with Richard Serra—his work, my work, the work of others, and just "work." It became apparent that Richard and I could sustain an interest in working together on some kind of issue, and I remembered the conversation with Pittas, which I recounted to Richard. He said, "Great! Let's do it."

I asked him what he would like to work on, what would interest him. He said he was interested in bridges—bridges as connections—bridges as objects. I had seen Richard's film on a bridge, and I realized that this is not the kind of project with which Richard is normally involved. The whole idea appealed to me on many different levels.

I applied for the grant and filled out the papers. At about the same time, I was contacted by The Architectural League regarding an artist-architect collaborative project. I told them about my own contemplated collaboration with Richard Serra.

Richard and I met at his studio with his associate Clara Weygeraf, who entered into our discussion and became our collective conscience. We spent the first evening leafing through books—Constructivism, Ledoux—ravenously searching for bridges and ideas of bridges to establish a basis for talking about bridges.

At the end of three or four hours we realized that everything was a bridge. That the books were a bridge between Richard and myself. And that, for a while anyway, we would keep the idea of bridges as open as possible. Before we left that night, we developed a strategy for working together on a bridge.

A while later, I was scheduled to present a one-week problem at Harvard. We decided to give the design of a bridge as the problem and to lure Harry Cobb into the week as another resource. It was hoped that the collective forum of the students and ourselves would involve everyone in an open discussion and focus on the bridge issue for one week. Out of this would come student projects and a lot of collective thinking.

Harry and I met the class on the first day and started showing slides, looking at books, much the same as Richard and I had on our first meeting. I met with the students the second day and tried to get them to focus on an individual project related to a bridge. Wednesday afternoon Richard arrived. He looked at what was being done and ripped into all of us, terrorizing the class as well as me. The students rebounded. It was an exciting twenty-four hours scrambling for ideas. Richard and I were in heavy discussions. What do you think of this person's work? What do you think of that person's work? Thursday afternoon Richard and I gave a joint criticism to the fifteen students. We told some of them to start over, and many of them did. They worked all Thursday night and made a final presentation on Friday to Harry, Richard, and me.

I have no idea what we accomplished. It was kind of an intensity of confrontation that I found exciting. I believe some of the students did as well. Harry Cobb perhaps understood what we were doing better than we did. Friday evening, after the final student presentation, Richard and I spiritedly discussed the student projects and found ourselves in agreement on which one was best. It happened to be the project of least interest to anyone else in the class. To me this indicated that at least Richard and I shared a similarly perverse attitude.

A lot of time passed between that meeting and our next work session. Both of us were traveling extensively in different parts of the country and

# Connections

*By Frank O. Gehry and Richard Serra*

found it most difficult to be in the same place at the same time. In the interim, two new large public projects of Richard's were built in New York, which dealt heavily with context and not connections. I was intensely involved with a house in California in which each room was a separate building. Though our projects had nothing in common, in retrospect I realize we were both avoiding "connections."

For our next session I made a special trip to New York to spend a day with Richard in his studio working on the League project. We needed to create a product that could be exhibited and included in a book and which addressed itself to the original problem of something functional.

Richard's studio window faces the World Trade Center. As we thrashed about looking for something upon which to focus, we decided on a project that joined two unlikely architectural objects: the World Trade Center and the Chrysler Building. That certainly poses problems of connections, both philosophical and pragmatic.

The idea became more and more stimulating. Clara, our conscience, came in time after time to pass judgment on the project, and she cast a skeptical eye. We couldn't stop. The connection of two unlikely objects of that scale persisted, and both of us started drawing ways in which such a connection could be made. Since it was Richard's studio, we worked with his tools. We made models in the sandbox and drew with solid paint blocks on huge sheets of paper—something I had never done before. The tactile quality of using those paint blocks on that kind of paper was tremendously satisfying and I was hooked.

During that process I discovered that although Richard was intrigued with the idea of connections, he had never dealt with it in the way we were required to on this problem. We had long discussions about the connection. How would it be accomplished? What would the engineering look like? What were the issues? As he grappled with that, I played with my new toy, the paint block.

The product of that whole day is what we submitted to the League. I don't know whether or not it has to be taken seriously at this point. Who cares about a connection between the World Trade Center and the Chrysler Building?

Well, we found—among the research material on bridges which we had been accumulating—a *New York Times* clipping. It stated that a bridge was completed in Hull, England, in 1980 that is the most expensive bridge ever built and the longest clear span. It's longer and even more repulsive than the Verrazano Narrows Bridge. So, in terms of bridges, this appears to be humanity's greatest expanse to date. The article went on to explain that this bridge joins two points which no one needs to go between. In this context, joining the World Trade Center with the Chrysler Building becomes a very practical proposal. If it were built, at least the people in New York could understand its existence and use it.

What happened between Richard Serra and me is certainly a beginning of mutual understanding. The project for The Architectural League is a start and not an end, and for that we are thankful.

I ran into Michael Pittas recently and asked, "How's our grant going, Michael?" He said, "You didn't fill the papers out right and it was rejected."
*Frank O. Gehry*

I have known Frank Gehry for several years. We have shared a mutual interest in sculpture and architecture and have been involved in an ongoing dialogue. Therefore the notion of a collaboration was that of applying a specific program to a shared concern. For the most part I find architects' theoretical pretension and self-serving polemics an enormous obstacle, but I have never found this with Frank. He has a candid, open, imaginative curiosity which doesn't make invention a dirty word.

Together we began to speculate and fantasize about the concept of a bridge. We started out with a very open idea about bridge building and ended up with the utopian idea of connecting the World Trade Center and the Chrysler Building. That concept has since been extended to actually connecting the internal structures of two separate buildings with a road in the sky. The concept of a bridge has been a catalyst for Frank and me to discuss many things beyond bridges, architecture, and art. We started our bridge connection long before we knew about The Architectural League project and we intend to continue. We don't take ourselves too seriously; we are not up to making a significant statement, yet.
*Richard Serra*

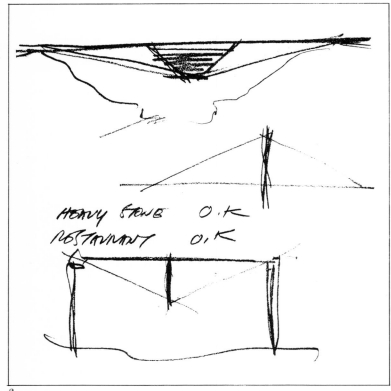

1

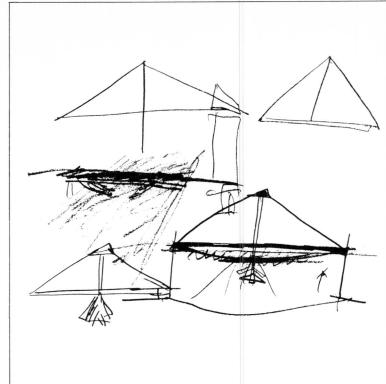

2

3

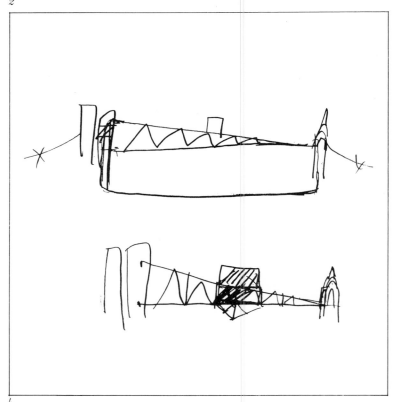

4

1 Bridge as a surrogate lock between two different water levels.

2 Having seen the work of a bridge builder in Düsseldorf who used one, two, or three pylons to support a cable system, we decided to explore this idea, but turn it around so that the cable was underwater. With this system, the bridge would be a freespan structure between the two land masses.

3 A further development of the same idea of the cable under the horizontal span with the possibility of including a building element as part of the structure.

4 In designing the bridge between the World Trade Center and the Chrysler Building, we incorporated some of our ideas gained in the exploration of the cable systems in the bridges in Düsseldorf. The bridge is connected into the structural system of both buildings, and a cable also connects the two structures underground. Because of the differences in height of the two buildings, the shape of the bridge is triangular or rhomboidal. There is the possibility of including an independent building within, above, or below the bridge span.

5

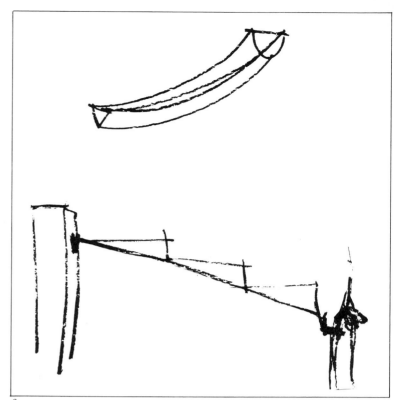

6

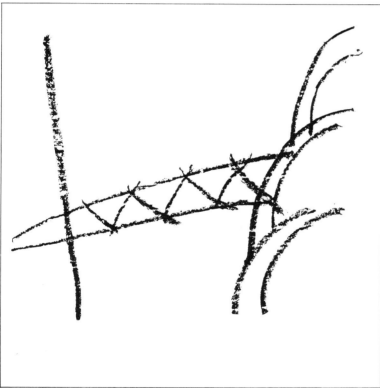

7

8

5–8  The sketches explore several methods of creating a bridge between two buildings of different heights and architectural styles. In one instance (7), the bridge structure penetrates the outer wall of the World Trade Center and connects into its structure. In another method (6), the bridge is floated between the two buildings and is joined with an independent structural connection. The curved sectional study of the bridge span has one triangular end and one semicircular end to accommodate to the two extremes of architectural style. The large triangular form (8) and the series of three stepped triangles (6) are two of the many shapes that such a bridge could take when connecting two structures at different points along their facades.

Modern public art in architectural contexts has by no means a predictable or assured future. Contemporary architecture and contemporary art alike have outlived the Modernist phase. Both, in quite different ways, are in periods of crisis and reassessment. American sculpture reached an apotheosis of sorts with David Smith—at least it has not dramatically improved upon his contribution; and contemporary American architecture isn't threatening to surpass the standard of Louis Kahn.

Thanks in large part to Alexander Calder, we all know what a contemporary abstract "public" sculpture looks like, but we're not quite accustomed to it in the way we are to modern architecture, for better or worse. With ambitious public and private building programs, modern architecture has become a part of our lives: consider the post-war evolution of such cities as New York or San Francisco, or more especially Chicago and the anomalous Columbus, Indiana. Contemporary public sculpture has a much shorter history and few real triumphs. Its achievements to date scarcely provide models for the future.

The history of the Modernist sculptural monument is simply too short to safely extrapolate and too tentative to provide genuine paradigms. In the recently marked absence of ongoing "Modernism" per se, all this amounts to a particularly haunting state of affairs. For Modernism came to heady fruition in American painting (and to a lesser extent in small- or medium-scale sculpture), and it blossomed and then waned in architecture. But in public sculpture, the Modernist impulse never did mature in fullness, and now it may already be obsolete.

In addressing the question of the future of contemporary public art and architecture, the issues of government money and government policy, which make it possible, are assumed to be the central ones. (Even though corporations and private foundations are increasingly involved in public art patronage, their role in American art on a massive scale is yet to be defined.) Artists and architects call for increased appropriations of public funds for mutual enterprises; the public meanwhile either watches impassively or experiences a sense of tax-paying resentment and moral confusion. But these things are really secondary to, or contingent on, deeper questions of aesthetic history and our own attitudes to this continuing dialectic. The attitudes which need to be examined aren't just those of the public who live with our urban environments, but of the architects and artists themselves who create

In recent decades and at present, public artworks resulting from artist/architect interaction can be divided into two basic kinds. The more common is the large-scale, more or less "abstract" sculptural object placed in a building lobby or outdoor public space. Often this kind of object is really nothing but an embellishment ex post facto to an architectural site whose whole conception barely took it into account. It is a sad commentary on the nature of collaboration that so much public sculpture does little more than plead mutely for a sense of identity. In its presence we feel a kind of helpless sympathy rather than any pleasurable acceptance, not to speak of edification. At best, such pieces in the "Modernist" tradition—the occasional Serra or DiSuvero or Noguchi—do stand as resonating artifacts of our contemporary aesthetic value system, correctly scaled to their environments and independently sufficient. The few very good ones *are* imposing enough, in that special decorative sense crystallized in late Matisse, that they transcend their environs. Or like the Oldenburg *Batcolumn* in Chicago or the secret Tony Smith *She* in Washington, they create a sort of Modernist anomaly achieving through sheer monolithism an inexplicable symbiosis between themselves and their surroundings. For in Modernism, any symbiosis—the quality of existence in radical harmony between object and surround—is in fact rarely a consequence of a prior intention, but instead relies on a stubborn unilateral exercise of artistic intelligence and luck in the final event. Lastingly successful results with this kind of large-scale public art are few and mostly accidentally achieved.

The other sort of collaborative public art is less familiar and less easily described as a single phenomenon. To use language borrowed from technology, it is heuristic (inherently problem solving) and systems-integrated. (It may be by

# Afterword

*By Jane Livingston*

definition Post-Modern.) It engages the artist in planning from the outset with architects and designers and builders, and can result in both practical and aesthetic solutions scarcely imaginable in our current primitive state of awareness.

Because of the expensiveness of significant art patronage, the whole history of architect/artist collaboration in the United States is bound up with institutional, generally governmental, intervention. The history of art and architectural collaboration sponsored by the National Endowment for the Arts (NEA) spans only fifteen years; and though rooted in the WPA of the 1930s, the General Services Administration (GSA) art program is similarly embryonic. Given their novitiate status, it is cause for optimism that both these agencies are moving in the direction of beginning their matchmakings between artist and architect in earlier rather than later stages of a site's development. Such catalytic acts of patronage might eventually result in an actual tradition of permanent works of art that are integral to their sites—works which use both natural and artificial light, building materials, accoustical properties, furnishings, and spaces themselves in ways which convey the best thought of the artist and, by influence, the best thought of the architect.

A prototype for collaboration in general—among artists, technicians, architects, and bureaucrats—took place more than a decade ago through the Los Angeles County Museum of Art's "Art and Technology" project.[1] Writing on the various kinds of artist/technician interchange that took place during this prolonged experiment, I noticed a striking paradox: in a situation full of new, sophisticated, and potentially intimidating technological challenges, the most difficult kind of collaboration between artist and nonartist (whether architect or technician) was the most traditional and ordinary one. Artists were completely undaunted by the exotic technologies they found in various California corporations, but they were exhausted and in some cases defeated by routine fabrication, owing to bureaucratic snags. At first we attributed the problem of making monuments to the clumsiness and inefficiency of old-fashioned industrial methodology. But we later came to see it

had to do with habituated attitudes. What stymied the artist's best efforts was never any esoteric technology, nor any mere clash of wills among various collaborators. It was something much more mundane and more immovable: it was simply the hazards of bureaucratic procedure which can so impersonally and implacably and infuriatingly disrupt a logical stream of activity. The corporations (this was not large government) plainly gave low priority to the various art projects; the artists had to forge their own way and make endlessly repeated demands. They ended by chalking it up to experience and opting for their own, often traditional, devices.

In the course of three years' involvement with scores of artists and corporations, we not only observed but suffered through the daily psychological reality of artist versus architect or engineer or scientist. The artists were by and large extraordinarily adaptable; if they finally gave up on a given project's realization, they shifted gears and worked productively with the situation of participation itself. Indeed a distinct phenomenon which I called a "participatory aesthetic" emerged in the course of the program.

By necessity architects are probably more resilient than artists in respect to bureaucratic reality. But ironically, they also often seem to be shockingly less practical than artists when it comes to either basic problem solving or complex deductive thought. Yet they are probably more patient than artists in the inevitable processes of testing and waiting. Ironies and contradictions pile up. The abyss between the utopianism of Modernist architecture and its theoretical notions of the practicable and the dismal realities of contemporary "planned cities" is poignant.[2] Contemporary architects of public buildings generally appear to approach their task with a virtually impossible combination of nominal altruism, economic conservatism, and inductive reasoning, so that in effect "the good" is predicted on wishful projection. Artists work quite differently: they tend to be more empirical in both little and big decisions and more impatient.

We might venture to conclude that the architect needs the artist more desperately than is true

1. Maurice Tuchman, *Art and Technology* (New York: Viking Press, 1971).
2. For a concise analysis of modern architecture's dilemma, see Peter Blake, *Form Follows Fiasco: Why Modern Architecture Hasn't Worked* (Boston/Toronto: Little Brown & Co., 1974).

conversely. A special paradox is at work here. Architecture as an art form, taken all in all, probably demonstrates more energy and more greatness than modern public sculpture; but the *sculptors* have often been the ones to dramatize the problems of both architecture and art, especially as they interact. In sum, it is the possibility of true cooperation—the subsuming of personal ego by both architects and artists in a larger effort, even while summoning will and inventiveness in the name of ultimate innovation—that must begin to concern us more urgently than it has until now.

The first step in a new symbiosis will be the willingness of the architect to receive the thinking of the artist. Such a radical shift could immediately free not just the architect but the whole system of commission and patronage. If artists and architects are engaged together at the outset of a given commission, funding and budgeting will be structured in ways clearly more advantageous to the entire aesthetic consideration of the situation than is true under our present system. It is fascinating to what extent at present our most audacious and sophisticated architects do categorically ignore the realm of contemporary art. (I suspect many of the so-called fantastic architects and others who claim artistic empathy delude themselves when they profess to be taking inspiration either from nonarchitectural art or from "systems aesthetics." Often the most artful architects are those who have the least direct contact with the world of self-conscious aesthetics.) There are exceptions: Philip Johnson and the Los Angeles architect Frank Gehry from the beginnings of their careers have used approaches and ideas inspired by good artists. The kind of aesthetic curiosity and aesthetic openness they exemplify may be more useful than ever in the coming years. If it is true that artists and architects probably share, if anything, *less* in terms of trained aesthetic assumptions and habits of thought than was supposed, they do, however, share one crucial attribute: both derive their greatest satisfaction from innovative solutions to the inevitable impasses encountered in the project of creating form. (This is not to say that we may not be entering upon a period of apparent conservatism, particularly in architecture, in which recycling will be an ascendant and healthy trend.) Moreover, architects and artists alike are understandably possessive of their viable solutions when they occur and self-protective when those ideas threaten to be co-opted without proper understanding or credit.

That the mind sets of the artists versus the architect are different seems clear, though it is not easy to analyze how or why. One hears well-developed opinions about motivational dichotomies from those who work with public art commissions. I've heard it said that architects are consistently more aggressive than artists in the imposition of their beliefs, both for good and for bad: they want not only the freedom to create and execute their ideas, but the luxury of converting the rest of us to them. The artist, however, in this argument, wants merely to be free to create and enabled to execute—but doesn't care about persuading others of his or her point of view. The artist wants in short to be left alone—though the testimony of many artists I know confutes this. And I myself observe that very often architects mistrust artists, and artists end up, if they do find themselves chosen in the collaborative situation, on one hand flattered and on the other frustrated because their opinions were solicited so late in the day.

In 1970, for the *Art and Technology* catalogue, Claes Oldenburg listed comparative attributes that distinguish the artist working alone in the studio from the same artist in a collaborative situation. Though the tone is certainly ironic, there is a distinct sense of longing for collaboration in Oldenburg's playful list. The isolated artist is alienated; the artist participating in the world is thoroughly adjusted and thoroughly useful to the universe (if in trade a little dehumanized):

| Artist in Studio | Artist in Collaborative Situation |
|---|---|
| intolerant | tolerant |
| rigid | flexible |
| stingy | giving |
| violent | restrained |
| vindictive-paranoid | forgiving |
| proud | self-effacing |

| Artist in Studio | Artist in Collaborative Situation |
|---|---|
| destructive (especially self) | constructive |
| compulsive | noncompulsive |
| drunk or high (looking for sublimity) | sober (indifferent to the sublime, like airplane pilots) |
| feverish | calm |
| alienated | participating |
| obsessive (primitive mind) | scientific |
| at ease | having difficulty[3] |

Of course there are many situations in which artist and architect ought never to be invited to collaborate. Artists are frequently asked to deal with hopelessly banal architectural spaces; and while within such a situation they might in some desultory manner help to enliven it, more often the shoddy environment kills everything within range, including the artist's best attempt to rescue it. One thinks of the Portman Omni Building in Atlanta, Georgia, versus the heroic and finally defeated Rockne Krebs. On occasion the opposite occurs; the architectural space has its own articulation and rightness and is disturbed or ruined by a boring or corny or inappropriate or even interesting "piece of art." The momentous proper placement of the right piece in the right place, then, would seem usually to happen either by sheer luck or by the astonishing occasions of mutual unselfishness between at least two talented people, dealing realistically with existing goods and evils. As has been stated already, both the NEA and the GSA are increasingly sensitive to the need in public art for early interaction between architect and artist. They want to start the process sooner and maintain contact among everyone as the project develops. Such questions as whether or not the architect, if he or she is selected as the first step, will be a voting member of the panel selecting the artist; or whether in some cases the artist ought to be selected before the architect; or whether alternately an already experienced team of artist/architect might be selected for a particular site remain to be answered.

3. Tuchman, *Art and Technology*, p. 269.

We are a long way from widespread, radically participatory architectural events.

But several collaborations of one sort or another (apart from those executed under the aegis of the present exhibition and publication) are now underway. In two presently developing cases—that of Nancy Holt in Rosslyn, Virginia (just across the Potomac from Washington, D.C.), and the new MIT Arts and Media Technology Building—the artists chosen are being given opportunities to influence architecture and landscape architecture. Holt has recommended and had approved building design changes in the not-yet-executed plan to accommodate her garden-area piece and is collaborating closely with the landscape architect. (The building architect in this case, perhaps significantly, is not interested in actual interchange with the artist and is not involved in the various planning sessions, at least at this point.) With the MIT building a somewhat different approach is being taken. The architect I.M. Pei is being called upon to work in various ways with six artists: Scott Burton is designing furniture; Dan Flavin, indoor lighting; Kenneth Noland, exterior surface color; James Turrell, natural lighting; Richard Fleishner, landscaping; and Alan Shields, entryway design. These two projects as they evolve will tell us a great deal about the dynamic of interchange between artists and architects; even more important, of course, in their implication for the future will be their ultimate aesthetic success or failure.

One might argue at this point, given our recent history, that architecture and sculpture cannot help but gain each from an openness to the other, whether or not they are matched early on. We must remember that in some ways artists and architects are united in purpose—for instance, in an urge to transcend that incredibly tenacious figure/ground dualism or to get beyond "objects" and "environment" and think in radical terms of space and human motions within it. And the public, who understandably has not always taken overnight to empty, looming, bombastic objects in forbidding spaces (namely, the wonderfully intended State University of New York campus at ·

Purchase or the Albany Mall), might appreciate a more subtle and sensitive approach to the aesthetics of communal spaces. In fact the best of several possible worlds may be achieved in Washington, D.C., in a situation which was in fact not conceived originally to incorporate a truly collaborative artist/architect interchange. The Old Post Office Building on Pennsylvania Avenue, built in the 1870s, is being reclaimed for use by two government agencies, the National Endowment for the Arts and the National Endowment for the Humanities. The architect Arthur Cotton Moore is at pains to preserve at least the most striking features of the building: its immense central atrium and tiers of flanking office spaces. The artist chosen to deal with the public space is Robert Irwin, who cannot be said to have been given the option of *collaboration* in any organic sense. But if any artist has a record of dealing with given situations according to the dictates of the whole problem, while still retaining his own special style and philosophy, it is Irwin. Again, this case will provide an important example through which to learn how to deal with a particular kind of situation—the artist working within a vast space and in a situation which involves renovation rather than new construction—which one hopes may become more and more frequent.

Of course many government or corporate buildings constructed recently are continuing in an inherently shortsighted way to provide for decorative art within their public areas, through various budgetary provisions—usually less than one percent of their cost. In these cases, the eventual addition of art is projected in initial planning stages but is not sought until the terminal phase. Unfortunately, such buildings are planned and built to self-destruct; in our free-enterprise system, we seem to be faced on all sides with planned obsolescence. Thus the artist is confronted with a building both functionally and aesthetically provisional and (often blessedly) destined for a short life span. (I admit to having served on NEA panels to choose sculptors for such buildings.) This factor, I think, encourages the creators of public sculpture to continue to think independently and opportunistically rather than entering a collaborative and long-range undertaking. Artists naturally enough want their solutions to make them look as good as possible, yet they can hardly be expected to surpass the sites given to them, especially if the site itself has a built-in obsolescence factor.

Finally, we should be reminded of the artistic tradition in which all this must be considered. We are not being gratuitously scornful of bureaucratic bad taste. For even in optimal situations, such as

the museum environment geared to displaying outdoor sculpture, the "public" work of art often seems provisional at best and grotesque at worst. Both the Hirshhorn in Washington, D.C., and the Whitney in New York provide examples of sadly off-the-mark solutions to displaying work in plain air: the Hirshhorn squats atop its sculpture mall while the Whitney relegates its outdoor objects to a moat. This is not to say that outdoor sculpture never works; when it does, the result can be so gratifying that we wonder how we lived without it. The Museum of Modern Art sculpture garden has entered into the acculturation of an entire urban and tourist generation: it constitutes an ineradicable prototype for a sort of urban oasis. This should be a vastly more widespread phenomenon than it is within the American museum context. (The new Baltimore Museum of Art sculpture garden may prove one more success in this particular genre.) But why we have so few truly intelligent and enlivening and comfortable sculpture gardens within American museums is a mystery, given the gifted artists—Tony Smith and Isamu Noguchi are between them a fabulous potential resource—who might be enlisted more productively than they have been.

Looking to the future, we might also ask ourselves if what we really want is more Rosatis and Meadmores and Sugarmans, more Bladens and Nevelsons; do we even want more Richard Serras and Tony Smiths and Michael Heizers, given the climate of misunderstanding and self-interest in which such works are created? Don't we need honestly to ask a little more both of our artists and of our architects, in the way of vision and thoughtfulness and concern for the people who will experience their creations? Certainly, they have not been given the best of possible circumstances in which to work, but what, finally, is cause and what result? If we can demand from our artists even more than we do now, well, then, of course we may emphatically demand infinitely more of our government agencies, federal, state, and local, to help subsidize and implement public art.

Probably we are entering a period of much greater tolerance on the part of the public for good, if sometimes initially mystifying, art—and more than this, a positive craving for livable and organically responsive architecture. Intelligent reclamation of existing architecture is a key to our aesthetic atmosphere in the coming era. But the really crucial issue is bound up with the good will toward one another, and the ability to think and feel authentically, on the part of both the creators and the patrons, in the name of better results than we have come to expect in our present system.

# Biographical Notes

## Emilio Ambasz

Born in Argentina in 1943, Emilio Ambasz received his Bachelor and Master of Architecture degrees from Princeton University. As the curator of design at the Museum of Modern Art from 1970 to 1976, Ambasz was responsible for such exhibitions as "The Taxi Project" and "The New Domestic Landscape," a show which provoked much discussion among professional and public audiences. A co-founder of the Institute for Architecture and Urban Studies in New York, he has taught both at Princeton's School of Architecture and Urban Planning and the Hochschule fur Gestaltung in Ulm, Germany.

The holder of numerous industrial and mechanical design patents, he is also the recipient of many design awards. Ambasz was awarded a fellowship from the Graham Foundation for Advanced Studies in the Fine Arts in 1969, and together with Giancarlo Pieretti, he shared in the Gold Medal Prize for Vertebra Seating given by the IBD in 1977 and the SMAU Prize in 1979.

The author of many articles, he was the editor of *Italy: The New Domestic Landscape* and *Think Program*, as well as the author of two books, *The Architecture of Luis Barragan* and *The Taxi Project*. His own design work has been featured in numerous international design publications, and he was one of the American representatives to the 1976 Venice Biennale.

## Lennart Anderson

Born in Detroit, Michigan, in 1928, Lennart Anderson studied at the School of the Art Institute of Chicago, the Cranbrook Academy of Art, and the Art Students League. He was a Rome Prize recipient from 1958 to 1961 and a Rome Prize Fellow at the American Academy in Rome. He has taught at Pratt Institute, the Art Students League, Yale, Columbia, Princeton, and the Skowhegan School of Painting and Sculpture, among other institutions. He is presently on the faculty of Brooklyn College.

The recipient of many awards, he is a member of the American Academy and Institute of Arts and Letters. Anderson's work is in public and private collections across the nation, including the Cleveland Museum of Art, Hirshhorn Museum and Sculpture Garden, the Minneapolis Institute of Arts, the Museum of Fine Arts in Boston, and the Whitney Museum of American Art in New York.

## Alice Aycock

Sculptor Alice Aycock, born in Pennsylvania in 1946, received her B.A. from Douglass College in New Brunswick, N.J., in 1968 and her M.A. from Hunter College in New York City in 1971. Her first one-person exhibition in 1972 at the Nova Scotia College of Art and Design has been followed in the last nine years by twenty-seven others at universities, galleries, and museums throughout the U.S., including a show at the Museum of Modern Art in 1977.

Aycock's work has also been included in numerous

group exhibitions, beginning with "26 Contemporary Women Artists" at the Aldrich Museum of Contemporary Art in Ridgefield, Connecticut, in 1971 and including the Biennale de Paris at the Museum of Modern Art in Paris in 1975; Documenta 6 in Kassel, Germany, and Artpark in Lewiston, New York, in 1977; "Made by Sculptors" at the Stedelijk Museum in Amsterdam and the Venice Biennale in 1978; and the Whitney Biennial in 1979. Aycock has been the subject of many reviews and articles in *Artforum, Art International, Arts Magazine,* as well as leading newspapers throughout the country.

## William Bailey

Born in Iowa in 1930, William Bailey attended the University of Kansas's School of Fine Arts and later received a B.F.A. and an M.F.A. from the Yale University School of Art in 1955 and 1957, respectively. An instructor and assistant professor in drawing at Yale from 1957 to 1961, then assistant and later professor of fine art at Indiana University from 1962 to 1969, Bailey returned to Yale in 1969 as an adjunct professor. He was appointed professor in 1973 and Kingman Brewster, Jr., Professor in 1979. Throughout his teaching career he has lectured extensively at universities and art schools across the country.

With over sixty-seven one-person, two-person, and group exhibitions to his credit since his paintings and drawings were first shown in 1956, Bailey's work has received considerable mention by U.S. and foreign publications, and he has been the focus of many feature articles, including several by Hilton Kramer in *The New York Times.* In addition, his work has been acquired for the permanent collections of many museums, including the Whitney Museum of American Art, the Hirshhorn Museum, the Philadelphia Academy, and the St. Louis Art Museum. Bailey has been the recipient of a Guggenheim Fellowship in 1965 and later a fellowship in painting from the Ingram Merril Foundation in 1979.

## Jonathan Barnett

Jonathan Barnett, AIA, AICP, is professor of architecture and director of the Graduate Program in Urban Design at the City College of New York, as well as an urban design consultant. President of The Architectural League of New York and a member of the board of the New York Landmarks Conservancy, he serves on the editorial advisory boards of *Process, Architecture* and *Urban Design International,* as well as on committees for major architectural schools. Author of many articles in professional journals and of two books—*Urban Design as Public Policy* and *The Architect as Developer,* with John C. Portman—Barnett has also chaired and spoken at many conferences and served as lecturer, critic, and juror at museums, galleries, and universities here and abroad. His professional work includes the master plan for the Gateway National Recreation Area in New York City, the Louisville Alley Study, and the Downtown Pittsburgh Development Strategy. Barnett was formerly the director of urban design for the City of New York, associate editor of *Architectural Record,* and project designer for Haines, Lundberg & Waehler, Architects, in New York City. Barnett was born in 1937.

## Jack Beal

Painter Jack Beal was born in Virginia in 1931 and educated at the Norfolk division of William and Mary College and the Art Institute of Chicago. He has had numerous one-person exhibitions at the Allan Frumkin Galleries in New York and Chicago, as well as a retrospective exhibition in 1974–1975, which traveled to the Virginia Museum in Richmond, Boston University, and the Museum of Contemporary Art in Chicago. Among the many group exhibitions in which his work has been represented were "Realism Now" at Vassar College and the "Whitney Annual" in 1968 and 1969, "22 Realists" at the Whitney Museum in 1970, as well as shows at the San Francisco Museum of Art, the Cleveland Museum of Art, the Akron Art Institute, the Milwaukee Art Center, and the Museum of Contemporary Art in Houston. Beal's work is part of the permanent collections of the Whitney Museum, the Walker Art Center, the Museum of Modern Art, the Art Institute of Chicago, and the San Francisco Museum of Art.

## Barbaralee Diamonstein

Writer, editor, television interviewer, and teacher, Barbaralee Diamonstein is a commentator on art and architecture. Special projects editor of *ARTnews* and *Antiques World,* she is arts and culture consultant to CBS-TV and to ABC Video Enterprises. Her column, "Women in the Arts," appears in the *Ladies' Home Journal.* She is a commissioner of the New York City Landmarks Preservation Commission, a member of the Board of Directors of the Landmarks Conservancy and the Municipal Art Society, as well as a commissioner for the New York City Cultural Affairs Commission. A former White House assistant and one-time director of cultural affairs for New York City, Diamonstein holds a doctoral degree from New York University. The recipient of a number of fellowships and grants, this year she is Van Day Truex Fellow of the New School for Social Research/Parsons School of Design, where she is conducting a series of videotaped conversations with photographers, entitled "Visions and Images: American Photographers on Photography." The transcripts of two previous series of her video interviews have been published in book form: *Inside New York's Art World* and *American Architecture Now.* Her other books include: *Open Secrets: 94 Women in Touch with Our Time, Our 200 Years: Tradition and Renewal, The Art World: 75 Years of ARTnews,* and *Buildings Reborn: New Uses, Old Places,* which was also the subject of a major national museum exhibit that traveled to a sixty-seven cities, of which she was the curator.

## Sondra Freckelton

Born in Michigan in 1936, Sondra Freckelton studied at the Art Institute of Chicago. Since 1959 when her work was shown in "Recent Sculpture U.S.A." at the Museum of Modern Art, Freckelton has had her work shown in over thirty exhibitions, including the Whitney Annual in 1964 and the sixth British International Print Biennale in 1979. Freckelton has had several one-person exhibitions at galleries in New York, Chicago, and Washington, D.C. Her work is included in the corporate collections of Best Products and the Prudential Insurance Company.

## James Ingo Freed

James Ingo Freed, FAIA, was born in Germany in 1930 and graduated from the Planning and Design Department at the Illinois Institute of Technology. He has taught and served as critic and juror for a number of other schools and competitions. Freed's designs for the National Bank of Commerce in Lincoln, Nebraska, and in New York, 88 Pine Street, Kips Bay Plaza Apartments, New York University Towers, and the New York City Convention Center have been highly acclaimed, and his work has been exhibited in Chicago, Minneapolis, and Finland, among other places. He is a partner with I. M. Pei & Partners in New York.

## Frank O. Gehry

A Canadian by birth, Frank O. Gehry, FAIA, received his Bachelor of Architecture degree from the University of Southern California and did graduate study in city planning at Harvard University. He has been a principal in his own firm, Frank O. Gehry and Associates, Inc., since 1963, and in 1979 he co-founded and is a principal in the firm of Gehry & Krueger, Inc., with offices in Los Angeles and Cambridge, Massachusetts.

While the Merriweather Post Pavilion of Music in Columbia, Maryland, won him an American Institute of Architects award in 1967— the first of ten AIA honor awards and citations he has received—it was his corrugated cardboard furniture designed in 1972 that first brought him wider public attention. Exhibited in the Musée des Arts Decoratifs in Paris and sold in Bloomingdale's in New York, it is also included in the design collection of the Museum of Modern Art.

Gehry has lectured at architectural schools throughout the U.S. He has been a visiting critic at Rice University, UCLA, and Cooper Union, and he held the William Bishop Chair at Yale's School of Architecture in 1979. In the 1980–1981 academic year, he taught at the University of Southern California, Southern California Institute of Architecture, and the Graduate School of Design at Harvard University.

## Paul Goldberger

Architecture critic Paul Goldberger received his B.A. in art history from Yale University in 1972 and joined the staff of *The New York Times* as an editor on its Sunday magazine. Appointed the architecture critic in 1973, Goldberger's articles and criticism on architecture, urban planning, historic preservation, and general design issues have appeared regularly since then.

Goldberger's feature articles have also appeared in *Art in America*, *Art News*, *Esquire*, *Horizon*, *New York Magazine*, and *Portfolio*, as well as in professional architectural journals. He is the author of *The City Observed: New York*, an architectural guide to Manhattan, and editor of the series of architectural guides, *The City Observed*. The writer of several introductions in the Global Architecture monograph series, he also contributed a major text essay to *Architectural Visions: The Drawings of Hugh Ferriss* and is currently at work on his second book, a history of the skyscraper. He is a member of the Board of Directors of the Society of Architectural Historians and of the Parks Council in New York City.

## Robert Graham

California artist Robert Graham, born in Mexico City in 1938, attended San Jose State College and the San Francisco Art Institute. Since 1964, his work has been shown in some forty-two one-person gallery exhibitions, ranging from California, Texas, and New York to England, Germany, and Switzerland. He has been included in many group shows, most notably the 1966, 1969, 1971, and 1979 Whitney Biennales in New York. His figurative sculpture is in the permanent collections of many major U.S. and European museums, including the Museum of Modern Art in New York, the Whitney Museum of American Art, the Pasadena Museum, the Hirshhorn Museum, the Los Angeles County Museum of Art, the Oakland Museum of Art, and the Walker Art Center. Abroad, his work is in the collections of several German museums, as well as the Victoria and Albert in London and the Museum of Modern Art in Paris.

## Michael Graves

Michael Graves, FAIA, was born in Indianapolis, Indiana, in 1934 and received his architecture training at the University of Cincinnati and at Harvard University. He was awarded the Prix de Rome in 1960 and studied at the American Academy in Rome for two years. Professor of architecture at Princeton University, Graves is widely known for the design of housing, cultural and institutional facilities, and town plans. He has won nine *Progressive Architecture* design awards and two National Honor Awards from the American Institute of Architects. He was awarded the 1980 Arnold W. Brunner Memorial Prize in architecture from the American Academy and National Institute of Arts and Letters. Graves's work is represented in numerous public and private collections, including the permanent collection of the Museum of Modern Art and the Cooper-Hewitt Museum. He was a U.S. representative at the XV Triennale in Milan in 1973 and a participant in the 1980 Venice Biennale. Since the 1972 publication of *Five Architects*, his work has appeared in many books and periodicals, the most comprehensive of which is a monograph published by Academy Editions in London in 1980.

## Richard Haas

Born in Wisconsin in 1936, Richard Haas received his B.S. in art and art education from the University of Wisconsin in Milwaukee in 1959 and an M.F.A. from the University of Minnesota in 1964. He has taught at the University of Minnesota and the Walker Art Center and has been an instructor in printmaking at Bennington College. In 1976, Haas was appointed to the Art Commission of the city of New York and served in that position for four years.

Haas's work as a painter began receiving recognition in the early sixties. He has had numerous one-person shows, including a retrospective in 1977 at the Norton Gallery of Art in Florida. His work has been featured in group exhibitions at museums and galleries across the United States and is in the permanent collections of many major U.S. museums.

Well known in the architectural world for his trompe l'oeil paintings, Haas has completed twelve of these wall murals since 1975, including six in New York City, the mural for the Boston Architectural Center, and his largest work to date at 1011 North LaSalle in Chicago. In recognition of his work, Haas received a medal from the American Institute of Architects in 1978.

## Hugh Hardy

Architect Hugh Hardy received his B. Arch. and M.F.A. from Princeton University in 1954 and 1956, respectively, and began his career as an architectural assistant to scenic designer Jo Mielziner in 1958. Four years later Hardy established his own architectural practice and was joined in 1964 by Malcolm Holzman and by Norman Pfeiffer the following year. Both Holzman and Pfeiffer were associates in 1966, and the partnership was established in 1967.

The firm is perhaps best known for its work on performing arts facilities and adaptive reuse projects, but it encompasses museum planning, housing, medical facilities, commercial development, and educational facilities. In addition to numerous design awards for individual projects, the three partners were recipients of the 1978 Medal of Honor given by the New York Chapter of the American Institute of Architects and the 1974 Arnold W. Brunner Prize in architecture awarded by the National Institute of Arts and Letters. The work of Hardy Holzman Pfeiffer Associates has been published extensively in professional journals here and abroad, has appeared in national magazines such as *Time* and

*Newsweek*, and was the subject of a feature article in *The New York Times Magazine*.

## Jane Livingston

Born in California in 1944, Jane Livingston graduated from Pomona College and Harvard University's Master of Fine Arts program. She is chief curator and associate director of the Corcoran Gallery of Art in Washington, D.C., where she has been since 1975. Before that Livingston was curator of modern art at the Los Angeles County Museum of Art. Formerly corresponding editor for *Art in America*, Livingston has written catalogues for many exhibitions and contributed to *Artforum*, *Studio International*, *Art and Artists*, and other periodicals. She has served as consulting panelist and museum policy advisor for the National Endowment for the Arts and chairman for College Art Association studio panels, and she is currently on the board of trustees of the Friends of Photography in Carmel, California, and Artists' Space in New York. Livingston has juried many exhibitions and lectured at galleries and colleges throughout the country.

## Richard Meier

Richard Meier, FAIA, born in New Jersey in 1934, received his Bachelor of Architecture degree from Cornell University in 1957 and established his own office in New York City in 1963. His best-known work includes single family residences, housing complexes, medical and cultural facilities, and commercial and industrial buildings. Several of his projects—notably Twin Parks Northeast Housing, Westbeth Artists' Housing, the Bronx Developmental Center, the Smith House, and the Douglas House—have received National Honor Awards from the American Institute of Architects; and his design for the recently completed Atheneum in New Harmony, Indiana, won a Progressive Architecture Design Award in 1979. Most recently Meier was the winner of an international competition for the design of the new Museum for the Decorative Arts in Frankfurt, West Germany. Among his other honors are the Arnold W. Brunner Memorial Prize from the National Institute of Arts and Letters in 1972 and the R.S. Reynolds Memorial Award in 1977. In 1976 he was elected to the College of Fellows of the American Institute of Architects and in 1980 received the Medal of Honor from the AIA's New York chapter.

## Michael Meritet

Born in New York City in 1948, Michael Meritet began his professional artistic career while serving in the U.S. armed forces in Viet Nam as a much sought-after portrait painter. Following his discharge, he continued his education at the State University of New York at Stony Brook and the School of Visual Arts in New York. In

1980 Meritet began collaborating on two projects with Emilio Ambasz.

## Charles Moore

Architect Charles Moore, FAIA, received his B. Arch. from the University of Michigan in 1947 and an M.F.A. and Ph.D. from Princeton University in 1956 and 1957, respectively. He began his teaching career at Princeton, where he was an assistant professor from 1957 to 1959 before becoming an associate professor in the Department of Architecture of the University of California at Berkeley from 1959 to 1965. Named chairman of the department in 1962, he also established his first practice in partnership with Donlyn Lyndon, William Turnbull, and Donald Whitaker in Berkeley that same year. Moving to New Haven in 1965 to become chairman of the School of Architecture at Yale University, Moore was chairman until 1969 and a professor until 1975, and he has been a visiting professor since 1976.

Concurrent with his teaching at Yale and ongoing practice in New Haven, Moore became a professor of architecture at UCLA in 1974 and architect in residence at the American Academy in Rome for the 1974–1975 academic year. Since moving back to the West Coast, he has been associated with two firms—Urban Innovations Group and Moore Ruble Yudell.

The recipient of many honors, Moore has won numerous design awards from *Progressive Architecture* and *Architectural Record* magazines, as well as countless national and local AIA honor and merit awards. Moore received a Guggenheim Foundation grant in 1977 and was awarded the Arnold W. Brunner Memorial Prize from the National Institute of Arts and Letters in 1979.

In addition to receiving coverage of his work in international magazines and in two monographs, Moore is a contributor of many articles to professional journals. Moore is also the author of several books, *Body, Memory and Architecture* (with Kent Bloomer), *The Place of Houses* (with Donlyn Lyndon and Gerald Allen), *Dimensions* (with Gerald Allen), and the soon-to-be-issued *The City Observed: Los Angeles*.

## Cesar Pelli

Born in Tucuman, Argentina, in 1926, Cesar Pelli earned a diploma in architecture in 1949 from the Universidad Nacional de Tucuman and later a Master of Science from the University of Illinois in 1954. Pelli was first associated with the firm of Eero Saarinen and Associates from 1954 to 1964 and then served as director of design of Daniel, Mann, Johnson and Mendenhall for four years before joining Gruen Associates in Los Angeles as partner for design. His design work for both these California firms gained him a reputation as a major architect in this country.

In 1977 Pelli became dean of the School of Architecture at Yale University. Since assuming his duties at Yale, Pelli has established his own office, Cesar Pelli and Associates, in New Haven, Connecticut. Among his many commissions, he is currently at work on the design of a major gallery expansion and residential tower for the Museum of Modern Art in New York City.

## Stephen S. Prokopoff

Stephen S. Prokopoff, born in 1929, received his B.A. from the University of California at Berkeley in 1951, his M.A. from the same institution a year later, and his Ph.D. from New York University in 1962. He was awarded a Fulbright grant in 1956 for study abroad. As an assistant professor of art at Skidmore College from 1961 to 1967, Prokopoff also assumed the duties of director of the college's gallery during the 1966–1967 academic year. Subsequently he has held similar posts as the director of the Institute of Contemporary Art at the University of Pennsylvania from 1967 to 1971, as director of the Museum of Contemporary Art in Chicago from 1971 to 1977, and currently as the director of the Institute of Contemporary Art in Boston. Prokopoff has combined his curatorial duties with teaching, first at the University of Chicago and now at Boston University.

Responsible for mounting the first major museum shows of such artists as Christo, Robert Indiana, Al Held, Robert Rauschenberg, Duane Hanson, and John DeAndre, Prokopoff also devoted time to exhibitions on architecture and crafts, including "100 Years of Architecture in Chicago" in 1976 and "Boston: 40 Years of Modern Architecture" in 1980. As the author of numerous catalogues to accompany exhibitions, Prokopoff has also written feature articles for *Arts Magazine* and *Art and Artists* and is the author of *The Nineteenth Century Architecture of Saratoga Springs, N.Y.*

## Vincent Scully

Born in New Haven, Connecticut, in 1920, Vincent Scully was educated at Yale University, completing his Ph.D. there in 1949. The Colonel John Trumbull Professor of Art History and master of Morse College at Yale University, Scully has been teaching there since 1947. He has written a number of important books on architecture, including *The Shingle Style: Architectural Theory and Design from Richardson to the Origins of Wright; The Earth, the Temple, and the Gods: Greek Sacred Architecture;* and *American Architecture and Urbanism.* In addition, he has worked on a number of films and television series on Egyptian, Greek, and American architecture and on the work of architect Louis I. Kahn. He lectures widely on the subject of ancient and modern art and architecture.

## Richard Serra

Born in San Francisco in 1939, Richard Serra

received a B.A. from the University of California in 1961 and a B.A. and M.F.A. from Yale University. Awarded a Yale Traveling Fellowship for a year of study in Paris upon graduation, Serra received a Fulbright grant the following year for study in Italy. Since his first one-person exhibition in Rome in 1966, his work has been exhibited widely, both internationally in Japan, Canada, England, Denmark, Germany, Holland, France, Italy, and Brazil, and nationally in such major museums and galleries as the Whitney Museum of Art, the Museum of Modern Art, Yale University, Los Angeles County Museum of Art, the Walker Art Center, the National Collection of Fine Arts, the Museum of Contemporary Art, and the Art Institute in Chicago. His work is owned by many private collectors, and is in the collections of major museums in North America and Europe. The subject of many reviews and feature articles, his work has appeared in *Artforum*, *Art in America*, *Art International*, *Arts*, *Domus*, as well as in *The New York Times*, *Newsweek*, and *The Village Voice*.

## Charles Simonds

Charles Simonds, born in 1945 in New York City, was educated at the University of California at Berkeley and received his M.F.A. from Rutgers University in 1969. Simonds has worked as an artist, in the streets of various cities for the past ten years, constructing dwelling places for an imaginary civilization of little people. He has had numerous one-person exhibitions, including ones at Centre Nationale d'Art Contemporain in Paris, the Museum of Modern Art in New York, and the Nationale Gallery in Berlin, and his work has been included in many group shows both here and abroad. The subject of many reviews and feature articles, Simonds's work has appeared in such publications as *The New Yorker*, *Art in America*, *Artforum*, and *Newsweek*. In addition to his work as a sculptor, he has also worked on six 16mm films.

## Frank Stella

Painter Frank Stella, born in 1936, studied painting first at Phillips Academy in Andover, Massachusetts, and later at Princeton University. Shortly after moving to New York, Stella had his first one-person show at the Leo Castelli Gallery in 1960, followed by successive shows there every two or three years since. In 1978 the Fort Worth Art Museum mounted the first retrospective of his work, "Stella Since 1970," which traveled this country and Canada for two years. Other retrospective shows include "Frank Stella Works 1953–1976," shown at the Kunsthalle Bielefeld in West Germany in 1977, and "Frank Stella Paintings, Drawings and Prints 1959–1977," held at the Knoedler Gallery in London in 1978.

Since 1959 his work has been included in major shows throughout North and South America, Europe, and Japan. Stella is represented in the permanent collections of many national and international museums, including the Hirshhorn Museum in Washington, D.C., the Whitney Museum of American Art, the Walker Art Center, the Art Institute of Chicago, the San Francisco Museum, the National Collection of Fine Art in Washington, D.C., the Tate Gallery in London, and the Stedelijk Museum in Amsterdam.

## Robert A. M. Stern

Robert A. M. Stern received a B.A. from Columbia University in 1960 and an M.A. from Yale University in 1965. A principal in his own practice since 1969—first with partner John Hagmann and later on his own—Stern has received many design awards, including one of four first places in the national housing competition for Roosevelt Island.

As prolific a writer as designer, Stern is the author of the exhibition catalogues, *40 Under 40: Young Talent in Architecture* and *New Directions in American Architecture*, and the book, *George Howe: Toward a Modern American Architecture*. He has been the co-editor of two issues of the Japanese architectural magazine *Architecture and Urbanism*, written many articles and book reviews for professional journals, and prepared the commentary for *Philip Johnson: Writings*.

As a teacher, Stern is currently an associate professor at Columbia University and has lectured extensively at schools and museums across the country. He has organized many symposia and exhibitions, and his work has been shown in several museums, including the Museum of Modern Art, the Cooper-Hewitt, and the Venice Biennale in 1976 and 1980.

## Stanley Tigerman

Stanley Tigerman, FAIA, was born in Chicago in 1930. He attended MIT and later received both his B. Arch. and M. Arch. from Yale University in 1961. In addition to running his own practice since 1964, he was a professor of architecture at the University of Illinois, Circle Campus, from 1965 to 1971, the 1979 Charlotte Davenport Professor of Architecture at Yale University, and architect-in-residence at the American Academy in Rome in 1980.

Currently on the Advisory Committee of the School of Architecture at Yale University, Tigerman was chairman of the AIA Committee on Design in 1976, a member of the Progressive Architecture Design Awards Jury in 1976, and chairman of the AIA Honors Jury in 1977. He has been the coordinator of several exhibitions in Chicago, the most recent of which was *Late Entries to the Chicago Tribune Competition*. In both 1976 and 1980 he was among the architects chosen to represent the United States at the Venice Biennale.

## Susana Torre

Susana Torre was born in Argentina in 1944, received her architectural degree from the University of Buenos Aires in 1967, and continued her postgraduate studies at Columbia University. From 1969 to 1971 she was associated with the Museum of Modern Art's Department of Architecture and Design as a Noble Foundation Fellow and was coordinator of "New Urban Settlements," a project of the Institute of Architecture and Urban Studies during 1970–1971. She has lectured about her work in over forty schools of architecture and has been a visiting design critic at several universities and colleges, including Yale, Syracuse, Nova Scotia, Cooper Union, and Pratt. From 1972 to 1976 Torre created and developed a nonprofessional architectural design curriculum at the State University of New York in Old Westbury, where she was an assistant professor and co-convenor of the Creative and Communicative Arts Program. She is currently an adjunct associate professor at the Graduate School of Architecture and Planning at Columbia University.

Torre's work as a practicing architect has been published in architectural magazines both here and abroad and has been shown in several gallery and museum exhibitions, including ones at the Cooper-Hewitt, the Museum of Modern Art, and the 1980 Venice Biennale. The recipient of a number of fellowships and grants, including one awarded by the National Endowment for the Arts for the study and design of housing prototypes for nontraditional families, Torre was a co-founder of The Architectural League of New York's Archive of Women in Architecture. From this initial idea, she later curated and designed the major traveling exhibition, *Women in American Architecture*, which opened at the Brooklyn Museum in 1977, and edited the book by the same title.

## Massimo Vignelli

Massimo Vignelli was born in Milan in 1931 and studied at Brera Academy of Art there and the School of Architecture at the University of Venice. From 1961 to 1965 he was a member of the Study Group of the International Council of Societies of Industrial Design, and in 1976–1977 he was president of the American Institute of Graphic Arts. Since 1973 he has been vice-president of The Architectural League of New York, and he is currently a trustee of the Institute for Architecture and Urban Studies.

Vignelli has taught at many design institutions in the U.S. and Italy. Besides winning national and international awards, he and his wife, Lella, were awarded the 1973 Industrial Arts Medal by the American Institute for Architects. Examples of his graphic and product design are in the permanent collection of the Museum of Modern Art, and in 1980 a major exhibition of the Vignellis' work was shown in the U.S. and Europe. His work is also well represented in internationally known design magazines and books.

In 1960 the Vignellis established the Lella and Massimo Vignelli Office of Design and Architecture in Milan, working in graphics, products, furniture, and interiors for major European companies and institutions, In 1965 Vignelli co-founded Unimark International, a corporation for design and marketing, of which he was a director and senior vice-president for design. Since 1971 he has been president of Vignelli Associates in New York, with liaison offices in Paris and Milan.

## Alice (Atkinson) Wingwall

Sculptor Alice Wingwall studied sculpture and architectural history at Indiana University in Bloomington, Indiana, the University of California at Berkeley, the Royal Academy of Fine Arts in Copenhagen, and Atelier Del Debbio in Paris. She received a Master's in sculpture from the University of California at Berkeley in 1963. She established a sculpture program for Wellesley College and taught there from 1973 to 1977. The recipient of a Graham Foundation grant, she traveled to Italy in 1977–1978 to photograph architecture and sculpture in small towns.

With architect Donlyn Lyndon, she designed the Hebrew Memorial Cemetery in Detroit in 1977, Project '70 for Boston, the gate for new dormitories at Pembroke University in 1975, and exhibition pieces, "Immanent Domains" of 1977, "Conceptual Urban Open Spaces" and "Elaborations of the Cooper-Hewitt Facade" of 1980. She is currently at work on the photographs for the book, *The City Observed: Boston*, and she has received a Design Arts grant from the National Endowment for the Arts for 1981.

# Illustration Credits

# Index